Matters of Mind

'This book aims to cut through the often obscure literature and reach the heart of the matter. Sturgeon has thought long and hard about the mind–body problem, and about the closely related topics of content and epistemological justification. Throughout he finds surprising but helpful new ways of laying out the issues. Rather than offering quick solutions, he seeks to identify the deep tensions which underlie current thinking. Because of this, philosophers of all stripes will find this a particularly helpful book. Even when he does not agree with some position, Sturgeon shows its proponents how best to understand it.'

David Papineau, *King's College London*

Matters of Mind is an exciting and challenging book that covers topical areas in the mind–body problem. Scott Sturgeon argues that most positions are overdrawn, that hardline views about materialism and dualism are unfounded. He offers a chapter-by-chapter analysis of various debates surrounding the mind–body problem, including visual experience, consciousness, content and norms, reliabilism and the problem of Zombies and Ghosts.

Matters of Mind will offer its readers a clear and careful exploration of the mind–body problem. It will prove an invaluable source to those interested both in epistemology and the metaphysics of mind.

Scott Sturgeon is Lecturer in Philosophy at Birkbeck College, London.

International Library of Philosophy

Edited by José Bermúdez, Tim Crane and Peter Sullivan

Advisory Board: Jonathan Barnes, Fred Dretske, Frances Kamm, Brian Leiter, Huw Price and Sydney Shoemaker

Matters of Mind

Consciousness, reason and nature

Scott Sturgeon

London and New York

First published 2000
by Routledge
11 New Fetter Lane, London EC4P 4EE

Simultaneously published in the USA and Canada
by Routledge
29 West 35th Street, New York, NY 10001

Routledge is an imprint of the Taylor & Francis Group

© 2000 Scott Sturgeon

Typeset in Times by
The Running Head Limited, Cambridge
Printed and bound in Great Britain by
Clays Ltd, St Ives plc

British Library Cataloguing in Publication Data
A catalogue record for this book is available from the British Library

Library of Congress Cataloging in Publication Data
A catalog record for this book has been requested

ISBN 0–415–10094–1 (hbk)
ISBN 0–415–23800–5 (pbk)

For Georgia Fay,
who taught by example

Contents

Acknowledgements

Many friends helped with the book. I am deeply grateful to them. As best I can reckon they are: Kent Bach, Mat Carmody, Dave Chalmers, Tim Crane, Marian David, John Divers, Doug Ehring, Miranda Fricker, Jen Hornsby, Jim Hopkins, Paul Horwich, Keith Hossack, Jon Kvanvig, Steve Laurence, Keith Lehrer, Brian Loar, Barry Loewer, Jonathan Lowe, Fraser MacBride, Genoveva Martí, Vann McGee, Sarah Patterson, John Pollock, Mark Sainsbury, Stephen Schiffer, Gabe Segal, Scott Shalkowski, Barry C. Smith, Wolfgang Spohn, Stephen Stich, Leo Stubenberg, Jon Sutton, Michael Tye, George Walker and Gene Witmer. Special thanks to the London crew: Dorothy Edgington, Mike Martin and David Papineau. And extra-special thanks to Maja Spener.

Bits to follow spring from articles I've published elsewhere. Chapter 1 corrects a good deal of 'Visual Experience', *Proceedings of the Aristotelian Society* (1998); Chapter 2 rewrites 'The Epistemic View of Subjectivity', *Journal of Philosophy* (1994); Chapter 3 draws on 'Rational Mind and Its Place in Nature', in Mark Sainsbury's *Thought and Ontology* (FrancoAngeli, 1996); Chapter 6 draws on 'Physicalism and Overdetermination', *Mind* (1998) and 'The Roots of Reductionism', in Barry Loewer's *Physicalism and Its Discontents* (Cambridge University Press, 2000).

Introduction

Setting things up

I ran across philosophy in 1985. The first thing to grip was the Mind–Body Problem. It looked asymmetric. Physics made our take on Body seem firm. Psychology didn't do that for Mind. My initial view – naïve of course – was that we needed to fix ideas about Mind. As I soon learned to put it: we needed a mark of the mental.

Brentano had one. He said the essence of Mind was its ability to represent. Aboutness was the key. The answer seemed apposite. It set out lines of inquiry and echoed the literature. Naturalizing Aboutness, after all, was then dominant in the profession. Hunting the seed of truth conditions occupied seminars across the country. Biosemantics had broken out on both sides of the Atlantic. Wisconsin had a view. The Mind–Body Problem looked clear. It was that of reducing Aboutness to Nature.

Times change. Today's tyro couldn't get that impression. The Problem looks too different. But its new face is no child of consensus. The once-deafening buzz of work on Aboutness has simply been replaced. The new cacophony springs from work on rather different topics.

This book reflects my view of what happened. Its chapters are organized and motivated by that view. So I begin with a thumbnail sketch. Consider a schema:

(*) 　　　　　X is About Y iff tokens of X stand in relation R to Ys.

Theories of this form used to be hot. They were the bedrock of work in the field. Their shift from the spotlight grew from five kinds of worry.

(1) When philosophers would cash (*) via some relation – R^* say – others would charge them with false advertising. They'd say R^* was intentional, its use in (*) did not service materialism. Naturalists would then argue for R^*'s *bona fides*. And to the extent they succeeded, critics would crank out the counter-example. They would insist putative reductions

of Aboutness were intentionally imbued or extensionally unfit. Naturalists would tinker with theory.

(2) Some philosophers emphasized an internal link between Aboutness and consciousness. Since nature could not edify the latter, they said, (*)-like views could not deal with the former. Their idea was that nature was mute *vis-à-vis* a crucial aspect of Mind's directedness on the world. It said nothing about *conscious* Aboutness. In a nutshell: the link between Aboutness and consciousness, plus the latter's theoretical recalcitrance, prevent reduction of the former.

(3) Others emphasized an internal link between Aboutness and normativity. Since one could not squeeze ought from is, they said, (*)-like views couldn't work. Their idea was that nature was mute *vis-à-vis* another crucial aspect of Mind's directedness on the world. It said nothing about *norms* of Aboutness. In a nutshell: normativity prevents reduction of Aboutness.

However, debate on this topic is full of confusion. There are two kinds of normativity in it. They often get run together. But we should respect their difference. We should insist on the distinction between *alethic* and *evidential* normativity. The former says

(T)   A term ⌜F⌝ should be applied to an object iff it's F.

The latter says

(E)   A term ⌜F⌝ should be applied to an object iff one's evidence indicates it's F.

(T) is a truth-based prescription. (E) is an evidence-based one. Truth and evidence come apart. The latter can mislead about the former. Alethic and evidential normativity are not the same thing. Viewed with a careful eye, though, discussion of content and norms can often be seen to run them together.

We should insist on two questions. One asks whether alethic normativity can be naturalized. The other asks whether evidential normativity can be. Naturalists tend to spin debate about normativity in terms of the first question. They emphasize their view about where truth conditions come from. They insist it leaves room for an alethic is–ought distinction. Non-naturalists tend to spin debate about normativity in terms of the second question. They emphasize difference of grain between truth conditions and epistemic possibility. They argue naturalism cannot account for content-based evidential norms.

(4) Some philosophers emphasized the fact that Mind and Body pull apart in conception. It's coherent to conceive one without the other. When

Body is conceived without Mind, Zombies are the topic. When Mind is conceived without Body, Ghosts are the topic. Their conceivability was used to argue for their genuine possibility. And that, in turn, was taken to show dualism is true.

(5) Others emphasized an empirical case for physicalism. Their idea was simple. Physics is closed and complete. Mind is causally efficacious. The world isn't choc full of overdetermination. It follows, they argued, that Mind is physical as well.

What does it all mean?

Well, note the first debate is one of detail. Nothing in it smells like principled difficulty for materialism. The issue is whether tight-enough fit can be found between Intentional and Natural phenomena. True, extant theories have problems, and we don't know how to solve them. But one thing is certain: at this stage in our intellectual development we have no real grip on whether, or to what extent, Mind and Nature correlate. We've no such grip on whether a thought relates to its truth conditions like a tree to its age, a bee dance to its target, smoke to its cause, or the disjunction of suchlike. All claims about that are highly speculative. This means proposed reductions of Aboutness are too. It also means all is to play for. The reasonable position to adopt – on the basis of category (1) debate – is Wait-and-See. Nothing in it forces the issue.

The other debates look different. They portend barriers to either materialism or dualism. One springs from consciousness, one from normativity, one from conceivability, one from science. *These* are the issues which now dominate philosophy of mind. And one can see why. They look to force the issue. They look to force a take on the Mind–Body Problem. I give each a chapter or more.

Chapter 1 tackles visual experience. This is where Aboutness and consciousness are most tightly wrapped into one. I make clear what a metaphysics of such experience might accomplish, and what constraints are in play during theory construction. I mark pros and cons of various positions and use them to construct a new view. One of the primary lessons of discussion is that an Explanatory Gap will exist between neutrally stated metaphysics and visual phenomenology. I discuss what that means for a reduction of Mind in general and Aboutness in particular.

Chapter 2 tackles the Explanatory Gap. I construct an exhaustive taxonomy of property explanation. Then I show why phenomenal properties cannot fit in it. I argue the nature of phenomenal concepts prevents them from figuring in pellucid property explanation. The Explanatory Gap has nothing to do with ontology. It's the product of facts about explanation and concepts. This means one of the putative barriers to naturalism is a fraud. The inexplicability of phenomenal Aboutness – indeed that of consciousness full stop – does not show Mind isn't matter. If a tight-enough correlation were found between consciousness and matter – a big 'if' to be sure – it would be reasonable to equate them despite the Explanatory Gap.

Chapter 3 tackles normativity of content. It reflects my dissatisfaction with extant discussion of content. That discussion is marked by two things at once: Fregean considerations of a distinctly epistemic nature, and divorce from working epistemology. That's got to be wrong. Frege invented modes of presentation to bridge the grainedness gap between truth conditions and epistemic possibility. Their *raison d'être* is epistemic. And recent work by Kripke, Putnam and Burge – canvassed in the chapter – turns Frege's gap into a chasm. Yet philosophy proceeds (all too often) as if epistemic norms and content are orthogonal topics. Chapter 3 explains why that isn't so. It begins by noting discussion of each topic has run in exact parallel within disjoint literatures. It then works towards an explanation of why. That explanation relies heavily on the notion of content-based norms. These are the norms many feel cannot be naturalized. The chapter plumps for an internal link between content and them.

Chapter 4 tackles naturalizing that normativity. I begin by distinguishing two types of probability. Process Reliabilism uses the first to reduce warrant to probability of truth. It's shown to be unacceptably insensitive to local evidential relations. The view is not properly content based. This motivates a position I call Content Reliabilism. It uses the second type of probability to reduce warrant to probability of truth. I argue the view can be shaped so that warrant springs from an activity that is both content-based and norm-guided. So shaped, the view captures much in our pre-theoretic take on warrant. I close with remarks on whether such a view is right.

Chapter 5 tackles Zombies and Ghosts. It contains an extended discussion of conceivability. I distinguish two kinds. One is grounded in conceptual coherence, the other in sensory imagination. I argue Zombies and Ghosts are both conceivable in the first sense. But only Ghosts are conceivable in the second. Only Ghosts are experientially imaginable. I also argue neither kind of conceivability is sufficient for genuine possibility. Hence the conceivability of Zombies and Ghosts does not establish dualism. It does, however, ground a *prima facie* case. For their conceivability is defeasible evidence for their genuine possibility; and this, in turn, is some reason to think dualism is true. When faced with it, materialists have two (compatible) options: either locate reason to defeat the evidence for thinking Zombies and Ghosts are genuinely possible, or deny such possibility implies dualism.

Chapter 6 tackles both strategies. It begins with the dominant empirical argument for physicalism: the Overdetermination Argument. As we've seen, the idea is that physicalism flows from three things: the causal efficacy of Mind, the causal completeness of physics, and the lack of overdetermination. The argument trades tacitly, though, on two notions of physical. One springs from everyday life, the other from microphysics. The trade results in fallacy. To correct it we need principles which push causation from everyday life into microphysics. I argue the alien face of that physics undermines our right to them. Our present understanding of matter calls into question the principles needed to patch The Overdetermination Argument. So there's a question: why has The Argument been so popular? I argue its popularity springs from reductive bias inherited from everyday life. Reflection on that bias shows the genuine possibility of Ghosts does not entail dualism.

Setting things aside

Much in this book prescinds from detailed metaphysics. To see why, consider two Mind–Body Problems. One concerns the relation between mental and physical types. The other concerns that between mental and physical tokens.

Mental types are properties. Relevant examples include the property of being in pain, the property of being queasy, the property of being drunk. Physical types are also properties (I count functional types as physical). Examples might be the property of C-fibres firing, the property of neurones being in spatial configuration N, the property of something being in spatial configuration N. The Type Mind–Body Problem concerns the relation between mental and physical properties. The question is whether they're radically distinct. Type dualism says *yes*. Type physicalism says *no*.

Mental tokens are events. Relevant examples include the onset of a particular auditory or gustatory experience. Physical tokens are also events. Examples might be a particular firing of C-fibres or shift of neural configuration. The Token Mind–Body Problem concerns the relation between mental and physical events. The question is whether they're radically distinct. Token dualism says *yes*. Token physicalism says *no*.

The details of all this depend on how properties and events are individuated, and how radical distinctness is defined. As everyone who's likely to read this book knows, however, the relevant literature is numbing. It sustains a never-ending tempest of debate. Four examples:

(1) Properties are said to be coarse-grained; fine-grained; abstract; concrete; built from actual extensions; possible extensions . . .
(2) Events are said to be persistent; momentary; built from temporal parts; indexed to change, subjects, times, locations, causes, effects, causes-and-effects . . .
(3) Radical distinctness of type is defined via strong, weak, global, local, logical, metaphysical, nomic supervenience; determinable–determinate relations; type identity . . .
(4) Radical distinctness of token is defined via part-whole relations which echo most everything in (3).

Individuating properties and events, like defining radical distinctness, is highly contentious. It demands a consensually unobtainable level of detail.

Luckily, we needn't pursue it. Our topics can be fully addressed with a pre-theoretic take on properties, events and distinctness. For instance, the key to Zombies is their lack of phenomenal consciousness. They threaten physicalism by combining the presence of physical features with the absence of phenomenal ones. The crucial issue – which crops up no matter how features are individuated – is whether this combination is possible. Similarly, the key to Ghosts is their lack of Body. They threaten physicalism by combining the presence of phenomenal features with the absence of non-phenomenal ones. Once more the issue is whether this combination is possible. Individuating features is by the by. Debate about dualism, Zombies and Ghosts should not turn on how features are individuated. That topic is much less clear than the debate itself.

The same point applies to the issues at (1)–(4). The Mind–Body Problem should not turn on property- or event-individuation, the modality of supervenience, or the interplay of such. Their details are much less clear than the Problem. Solutions to it which turn on such issues preach deservedly to the converted. For this reason, I shun detailed metaphysics wherever possible in this book.

I also keep scholarly citation to a minimum. The book covers a great many topics. Regular footnotes with commentary render it indigestible. Trust me. I've tried it both ways. Things are much better with Discussion Points at the end of each Chapter. They cover side issues which merit discussion. They cite a good deal of relevant literature.

And finally: the book as a whole recommends a view on the Mind–Body Problem. But its line is suppressed until the end. Chapters 1 to 6 argue for non-trivial results in their own areas. In turn those results jointly support a take on the Mind–Body Problem. But I leave the big picture to the Conclusion. Only it rests on what it follows. This has good and bad knock-on effects. On the good side: chapters can be read in any order. They can also be studied in isolation. Interest in them does not require interest in the Mind–Body Problem. Hence the book should appeal to many not directly vexed by that Problem. On the down side: there is less surface-level unity in what follows than normally found in a monograph. This is intentional, of course, but it can unsettle. I hope the pros outweigh the cons of my strategy.

Chapter 1

Visual experience

1.1 Three types of visual experience

Suppose you see a cloud pass by. The cloud is a publicly available object of perception. Everyone can see it. Suppose the cloud looks white to you; and suppose that's because it is white. In the event, an instance of

(L)   It looks to you as if something is F

is made true by an instance of

(V)   An F public object looks F to you.

It looks to you as if something is white because a white public object looks white to you. Your visual experience is both trustworthy and accurate. You enjoy the first type of visual experience: *veridical perception*.

Suppose, however, you see a straight stick partially submerged in water. The stick looks bent. Here too we have an instance of (L): it looks to you as if something is bent. But this instance of (L) is not made true by a salient instance of (V). No bent public object looks bent to you. Rather, this instance of (L) is made true by an instance of

(I)   A *non*-F public object looks F to you.

A non-bent public object looks bent to you. Your visual experience is not fully trustworthy, not fully accurate. You suffer the second type of visual experience: *illusion*.

Finally, suppose drugs make it look as if a ball hovers in mid-air. This instance of (L) is made true neither by a salient instance of (V), nor by such an instance (I). No public object looks to you as if it hovers. We may assert the salient instance of

(H)   No public object looks F to you.

Your visual experience is untrustworthy. You suffer the third type of visual experience: *hallucination*.

There are three types of visual experience: veridical perception, illusion and hallucination. To a rough first approximation: veridical perception cottons onto public objects and their features; illusion does the former without doing the latter; and hallucination, somehow, does neither. Despite these obvious differences: veridical perception, illusion and hallucination share five Remarkable Features. My first task is to expose them. Then I'll work towards the view of visual experience which best explains them.

1.2 Five Remarkable Features

Suppose you're standing in a field on a bright sunny day. Your vision is good, you know that, and you've no thought to distrust your eyes. A friend shouts from behind. You turn. It looks as if a rock is flying at your face. You wish not to be hit. In the event, five things are clear.

First: you'll come to believe a rock is flying towards you on the basis of how it looks, that belief will join with your desire not to be hit, and the two will cause you to duck. The pattern is integral to common sense: when it looks to someone as if something is flying at them, and they wish not to be hit, then (*ceteris paribus*) they'll come to believe they're about to be hit and try to duck. This much is obvious. But notice: it prescinds from which *type* of look state they enjoy. It prescinds from whether it's a veridical perception, illusion or hallucination. That detail is irrelevant. As far as belief formation and action are concerned, the same immediate downstream effects are made likely by all three. Common sense sees them as driving belief and action in parallel. I signal this by saying they are

[1]   Behaviourally Equivalent.

Second: your belief and action are reasonable. After all: it looks to you as if a rock is flying at your face, you wish not to be hit, you've no thought to distrust your eyes, the setting is normal, the lighting is good, you know all this to be true. In an *important* sense of rational, common sense suggests your belief and action are rational. It does so, however, without knowing whether your visual experience is veridical, illusory or hallucinatory. Once more the detail is irrelevant. Common sense sees them as rationalizing belief and action in parallel (in the relevant sense). I signal this by saying they are

[2]   Rationally Equivalent.

Third: your visual experience will be subject to intuitions which form our conception of phenomenal consciousness. Specifically:

(I1)	There's something it's like for you when it looks as if a rock is flying at your face.
(I2)	To understand this visual state fully one must know what it's like.
(I3)	To know what it's like one must have enjoyed this kind of visual state (or, failing that, a similar kind of visual state).

Consider how plausible it is that congenitally blind people do not understand visual experience. Consider how little talking can teach them. They lack a required ingredient of understanding: viz., visual experience itself. (I1)–(I3) explain this. But they do so, notice, without knowing whether visual experience is veridical, illusory or hallucinatory. Common sense sees them in terms of (I1)–(I3). I signal this by saying they are

[3]   Subjective.

Fourth: your visual experience will place a moving rock before the mind in a uniquely vivid way. Its phenomenology will be as if a scene is made manifest to you. This is the most striking aspect of visual consciousness. It's the signal feature of visual phenomenology. And there's nothing ineffable about it. Such phenomenology involves a uniquely vivid directedness upon the world. Visual phenomenology makes it for a subject as if a scene is simply presented. Veridical perception, illusion and hallucination seem to place objects and their features directly before the mind. I signal this by saying they are

[4]   Scene-Immediate.

Fifth: you cannot tell, merely by inspecting phenomenology, whether your visual experience is veridical, illusory or hallucinatory. All three types of visual experience are 'indistinguishable from within'. Merely reflecting on what it's like will not tell you which sort of look state you enjoy. This does not mean you cannot tell which sort of state you're in. It just means your capacity to do so relies on background assumptions about your environment. Phenomenology alone will not tell you. I signal this by saying veridical perception, illusion and hallucination are

[5]   Indistinguishable.

In sum: veridical perception, illusion and hallucination share five Remarkable Features. They are Behaviourally Equivalent, Rationally Equivalent, Subjective, Scene-Immediate and Indistinguishable. It's of first importance to note, however, that these are *pre*-theoretic facts about visual experience.

They're no part of views concerning the nature of such experience. Rather, they constrain such views. For they motivate

> *Question 1*: Is there a common factor to veridical perception, illusion and hallucination which explains [1]–[5]?

1.3 Disjunctive Quietism

There's no guarantee Question 1 takes *yes*. Perhaps veridical perception, illusion and hallucination have nothing in common other than Remarkable Features. Perhaps they share nothing to explain their common functional/ normative nature. The thought is not incoherent. But accepting it, without being forced to do so, is methodologically unsound. [1]–[5] motivate unifying the phenomena. And the point is non-negotiable: unified theory trumps disunified theory or no theory at all. It's always better to have unified theory when possible. And as we'll see in §1.8, it's possible to unify [1]–[5].

This point threatens an increasingly popular approach to visual experience. I call it Disjunctive Quietism (or Disjunctivism for short). The approach is a three-part invention.

Part 1 characterizes visual looks with a disjunction:

(D)   X is a look as if ∅ iff either
(v)   X is a veridical perception of the fact that ∅; or
(i)   X is an illusion as if ∅; or
(h)   X is an hallucination as if ∅.

This, of course, is true. Visual experience comes in three flavours. Everyone should believe (D).

Part 2 denies veridical perception, illusion and hallucination share an underlying nature. This is done by sketching truth-makers for (Dv)–(Dh). Those for (Dv) receive the direct-acquaintance treatment:

(Dv) (1)   Veridical perception consists in brute acquaintance between percipient, public object and public-feature. This relation is object- and feature-involving, and cognitively primitive. It does not decompose into more elementary mental ingredients.
      (2)   Instances of direct acquaintance are phenomenally typed by their public-feature *relata*. Two veridical experiences are phenomenally type identical iff they spring from instances of identical public features.

In a nutshell, then, veridical perception is an instance of brute acquaintance between percipient, public object, and public feature; and such perception is of phenomenal type F_A when F is the feature with whose public instance a percipient is brutely acquainted.

Truth-makers for (Di) and (Dh) are sketched relative to this gloss. Those for illusion receive partly positive, partly negative treatment:

(Di) (1) Illusion consists in brute acquaintance between percipient and public object.

(2) Illusory phenomenology is not typed by public-feature *relata*.

And those for hallucination receive purely negative treatment:

(Dh) (1) Hallucination does not consist in brute acquaintance with public objects (or public features).

Disjunctivism's metaphysics of veridical perception and illusion is built atop brute acquaintance with public objects. Its metaphysics of hallucination is not. The view marks from the outset that two of three types of visual experience are perceptual states. Their public-object-involving nature makes them perceptual contact with the world. This ready-made division is both right and proper.

Part 3 involves the lack of support commentary (from whence the view's name). In particular: we have no positive story about the phenomenology of illusion, and no positive story about hallucination at all. Disjunctivism asserts (D), denies a common thread runs through its right-hand side, and then remains studiously silent.

This is no good. Full-dress theory should unify the phenomena or explain why it cannot be done. In the present context, such theory should explain Remarkable Features or make clear why they cannot be explained. Disjunctivism does neither. But we should consider how it might try to do so. This will make clear that the view's explanatory potential springs from resources available to other positions. It will also show what a theory of visual experience might hope to accomplish. In turn that will help us construct a view which unifies the phenomena.

Indistinguishability

Disjunctivism contains a metaphysics of phenomenal properties in the veridical case. It individuates them in a public-feature-involving way. For this reason, it cannot say those properties are present in delusion. Their presence requires that of real-world features definitionally unrequired by delusion. Example: the view must deny the phenomenal property present when one veridically perceives a bent stick is also present when one suffers an Indistinguishable illusion as of a bent stick. The veridical phenomenal property is individuated via bentness. One needn't be aware of genuine bentness when suffering an illusion as of a bent stick. The veridical phenomenal property is thus absent when so suffering. Disjunctivism must deny Indistinguishable veridical perception, illusion and hallucination are phenomenally type-identical.

When introspecting the phenomenal nature of visual states, Disjunctivism says we *just miss* phenomenal differences which set apart veridical perception, illusion and hallucination. It says illusions and hallucinations differ phenomenally from their veridical cousins. We just miss the difference. Indistinguishability is incapacity on our part. Everyone agrees about that. But Disjunctivism denies it grows from phenomenal type-identity on experience's part. Rather, it says inability to detect phenomenal difference prevents introspecting the genuine contours of our phenomenal life. Inability to detect phenomenal difference prevents introspecting the true nature of experience. When it comes to explaining Indistinguishability, then, the view simply takes it for granted and denies it springs from phenomenal type-identity.

Keep in mind, however, that Introspection is not inner vision. When introspecting what a visual state is like, we form judgements about the visual state directly on its basis. Introspection is one type of belief formation. The beliefs so formed are about visual states. But their formation does not spring from inner visual impressions of those visual states. There are no inner meta-visual states. Introspective beliefs about visual states spring directly from visual states themselves. To say two such states are Indistinguishable, then, is to say they register equivalently in Introspection. It's to say when judgements about them are formed directly on their basis, those judgements characterize them in the same way. It's to say Introspection run on them yields equivalent beliefs about them. Keeping this point in focus greatly aids in the perception of Disjunctivism's weaknesses. For it shows Indistinguishability cannot usefully explain other Remarkable Features.

Scene-Immediacy

This is without question the truly amazing Feature of visual experience. It's also the most difficult to handle. We should reflect carefully, then, on the fact that many feel Disjunctivism is uniquely well placed to do so. They say its capacity to explain Scene-Immediacy springs from its metaphysics of veridical phenomenology. According to that story, recall, such phenomenology consists in brute contact between percipient, public object and public feature. Scene-Immediacy is said to result. The idea is that brute contact makes it for the subject as if a public object and its features are directly before the mind.

Many feel this is easily the best account of Scene-Immediacy. 'After all', they say, 'that's just how visual phenomenology strikes us.' Indeed some go so far as to say the view's positive metaphysics is required to make sense of Aboutness. In McDowell's memorable phrase, something like Disjunctivism is required to understand 'subjective postures with objective purport' (McDowell 1997: 335–6, 1994 and 1986; the view is enthusiastically seconded by Putnam 1994).

I put no stock in this line. Suppose S veridically perceives O is F. Then we have

(1)   The phenomenology of S's experience will be as if O and its Fness are directly presented.

S's experience will be Scene-Immediate. Disjunctivism says (1) is true because

(2)   S enjoys brute acquaintance with O and its Fness.

And it adds such contact is object- and feature-involving and unbuilt from mental ingredients. Certain philosophers express this in other words. Some say (1) is true because

(3)   The fact that O is F manifests itself to S.

Others say (1) is true because

(4)   O and its Fness appear to S.

But the basic idea is clear: S enjoys Scene-Immediacy because she's in brute contact with O and its Fness.

Now, a quick glance at the story shows it has the right shape and feel. This surface impression generates the oft-vocalized view that Disjunctivism is uniquely well placed to explain phenomenology. But the impression should be resisted. For stripped of ideology (2)–(4) amount to no more than this:

(*)   S, O and its Fness stand in a relation, R, which is object- and feature-involving and unbuilt from mental ingredients.

R takes many names, as we've seen. But only God knows why it *deserves* them. And therein lies the rub.

Disjunctivism's celebrated explanatory punch springs from ideology. Yet that ideology is pulled from thin air. The view relies on phenomenal notions in its approach to phenomenology. It does not explain their origin, applicability or explanatory role. Think of it this way. Suppose S, O and its Fness stand in an object- and feature-involving relation unbuilt from mental ingredients. Does it *follow* any of (2)–(4) are true? Of course not. There are countless (*)-like relations definable. Most have nothing to do with Scene-Immediacy. Aside from its connection to such Immediacy, however, the *only* thing we know about *R* is it's (*)-like. And that's not much to go on. It's certainly not enough to secure a phenomenal name. Disjunctivism's ideology is pulled from thin air.

One might conclude the view has no explanatory punch after all. Perhaps its reliance on loaded ideology undercuts its capacity to explain phenomenology. Celebrated appearances to the contrary, one might say, spring from notational sleight of hand. But that would be overreaction. For it's not apriori that Scene-Immediacy grows from object- and feature-involving phenomena. If so, that's news. Nor is it apriori that such Immediacy is unbuilt from mental ingredients. If so, that too is news. It's unclear (1) grows from anything like (*). The view's *spiel* has non-trivial content. It just wraps that content in notions suffused with phenomenal connotation. Hence the view can seem profound one moment and trivial the next.

This is no blemish. There's a large and well-known Explanatory Gap between phenomenal states and all else. It will be the subject of the next chapter. For now we note merely this: *no* story told in non-phenomenal terms can explain the existence of phenomenology. No such story can explain Subjectivity. To bridge the Gap between (*) and (1), therefore, *R* requires phenomenal gloss. No surprise (2)–(4) creep into the literature. Something like them is needed. (*)'s metaphysics cannot render Scene-Immediacy pellucid. No such story can. Through its use of (2), then, Disjunctivism does two things. It tags such Immediacy with a canonical label. And it yokes non-trivial metaphysics to its tag. The same goes for (3) and (4).

This is important. The impression Disjunctivism is uniquely well placed to explain visual consciousness is mistaken. It results from a glance at the view's metaphysics with Scene-Immediacy in the back of one's mind. Since the two have the same basic shape, one might think the former is especially apt to explain the latter. But the thought does not withstand scrutiny. Their shape, after all, is too easy to have. It's had by all manner of complex relations. Disjunctivism has little more than a label for Scene-Immediacy. And what more it does have is (*). Like all non-phenomenal stories, however, (*) generates an Explanatory Gap. It does not fully explain phenomenology. It yields no deeper insight into Scene-Immediacy than can be got from other stories on offer. The sense it provides more is due entirely to ideology.

Every full-dress theory of visual experience splits into two parts: a neutral metaphysics and a phenomenal gloss. Without the latter, a view would look hopeless. The Explanatory Gap guarantees that. Without the former, a view would look vacuous. Philosophical demand guarantees that. Disjunctivism has both components. It should not be slapped down for that. But other views can do so as well. They too can spice metaphysics with phenomenal gloss. The Gap leaves no other option. For this reason, however, Disjunctivism is no better placed to explain visual phenomenology than other live options. It does what all decent views must do. It links such phenomenology with metaphysics of an intuitively right shape, and it glosses the link in phenomenal terms. But it does no more. The view defended in §1.8 does exactly as much.

Further still, Disjunctivism is unable to account for delusive Scene-Immediacy. For the only resource it might use to explain this Feature is Indistinguishability. Yet the attempt to do so fails. Consider Macbeth's dagger. The Indistinguishability-based explanation of its Scene-Immediacy says:

(A)   Macbeth's hallucination is Scene-Immediate

because

(B)   it's Indistinguishable from a matching Scene-Immediate veridical perception as of a dagger.

This account of delusory Scene-Immediacy just doesn't work. In no good sense of explanation does the (B)-to-(A) story deserve the label. After all, how could Macbeth's Scene-Immediacy spring from his inability to introspect the difference between delusory experience and phenomenally distinct veridical perception? Remember, that's all Indistinguishability comes to. How then could it be for Macbeth as if a dagger is directly before his mind merely because he cannot detect real phenomenal differences between his experience?

It's trivial, of course, that Macbeth is inclined *to think* it is for him as if a dagger is directly before his mind. That follows from Indistinguishability by definition. Given his hallucination is Indistinguishable from a Scene-Immediate veridical perception, it follows analytically that Macbeth is disposed to believe (on the basis of introspection) his experience is phenomenally like the veridical perception. But it's one thing to think an experience has a property and another for it to do so. Indeed the difference is fundamental to Disjunctivism. It's built on the thought we're disposed to form false introspective beliefs about delusive phenomenology. The question is sharp: how could it *genuinely be* for Macbeth as if a dagger is directly before him merely because he's disposed to think it so?

I say it could not. It could not genuinely be for him as if a dagger is directly before him merely because he's disposed to form false beliefs about what delusion is like. Capacity-like (B) facts wear a different face than fabric-of-experience-like (A) facts. The former do not explain the latter. They do not have the right shape. As a result, Indistinguishability cannot ground Scene-Immediacy. When it comes to explaining that Immediacy, then, there are two cases to consider: veridical and delusive experience. Concerning the former, Disjunctivism provides a grip enhanced by pretheoretic understanding. Concerning the latter, it provides no grip at all.

Subjectivity

Disjunctivism can begin to say why veridical perception and illusion are Subjective. For it claims they're relations of acquaintance. Yet common sense already views such relations in Subjective terms. Consider a pair of examples:

> Suppose you knew Paris through having lived there. You were acquainted with the city. Then, I submit, there was something it was like for you to know Paris as you did. But to understand that properly, one must know what it was like for you. To know *that*, however, one must live in Paris (or somewhere similar). This much is common sense. Yet it's exactly in line with Subjectivity. Think of our conversation after your return. Having never travelled, I ask what it was like being in Paris. (If I'd been there I would've asked what you did, not what it was like. I'd already more or less know what it was like.) I assume there was something it was like. I want to know what it was like. You describe walking the Tuileries, exploring the Louvre, busking in Montmartre. Eventually you give up. You cannot explain what it was like. You can hint, gesture, spin the odd analogy. But you can't get me to know by talking. If I really want to know what it was like to be in Paris, I should go there.

> Suppose you knew jungle warfare through having fought in Vietnam. You were acquainted with the phenomenon. Then, I submit, there was something it was like for you to know war as you did. But to understand that properly, one must know what it was like. To know *that*, however, one must fight in the jungle (or somewhere similar). Again this is common sense. Yet it's exactly in line with Subjectivity. Think of our conversation after your return. Having never fought a war, I ask what it was like. I assume there was something it was like. I want to know what it was like. You describe sleeping in the jungle, search and destroy missions, body counts. Eventually you give up. You cannot explain what it was like. You can hint, gesture, spin the odd analogy. But you can't get me to know by talking. If I really want to know what it was like, I should go fight.

Common sense views acquaintance relations in line with (I1)–(I3). It already subjects acquaintance-based knowledge to these intuitions. For this reason, Disjunctivism can say something non-trivial about the Subjectivity of veridical and illusory experience. It need only appeal to our ordinary take on acquaintance plus its view that such experience is a type of acquaintance.

Having said that, the view is unable to account for hallucinatory Subjectivity. For the only resource at its disposal to explain this Feature is Indistinguishability. Yet the attempt to do so fails. Just consider Macbeth's dagger. The Indistinguishability-based explanation of its Subjectivity says:

(A)   Macbeth's hallucination is subject to (I1)–(I3)

because

(B)   it's Indistinguishable from a matching veridical perception as of a dagger which is so subject.

This account of hallucinatory Subjectivity just doesn't work. In no good sense of explanation does the (B)-to-(A) story deserve the label. After all, how could Macbeth's Subjectivity spring from his inability to detect genuine differences between hallucinatory experience and phenomenally distinct veridical and illusory experience? Remember, that's all Indistinguishability comes to. How then could (I1)–(I3) apply to Macbeth's experience merely because he can't detect real phenomenal differences among his experience?

It's trivial, of course, that Macbeth is inclined *to think* his experience is Subjective. That follows from Indistinguishability by definition. Given his hallucination is Indistinguishable from a Subjective veridical perception, it follows analytically that Macbeth is disposed to believe (on the basis of introspection) his experience is the same. But it's one thing to think an experience has a property and another for it to do so. The question is sharp here as well: how could Macbeth's experience *genuinely be* Subjective merely because he's disposed to think it so?

I say it could not. Capacity-like (B) facts wear a different face than fabric-of-experience-like (A) facts. The former do not explain the latter. They do not have the right shape. As a result, Indistinguishability cannot ground Subjectivity. When it comes to Subjectivity, then, there are two cases to consider: visual perception and hallucination. Concerning the former, Disjunctivism has a nice story based on acquaintance. Concerning the latter, it has no decent story at all.

Rational Equivalence

Disjunctivism can say why veridical perception warrants belief and action. And it can do so, importantly, to the mutual satisfaction of internalists, externalists and common sense. Since Disjunctivism is the only theory which can do that, I'd like to get clear on the point.

Internalists say reason springs from that to which agents have immediate access. Externalists say reason springs from truth (or truth-oriented features like reliability). Disjunctivism says veridical perception consists in the immediate access to truth. It generates a story about such perception's capacity to rationalize belief and action. That story is kosher by internalist and externalist lights:

Disjunctivism's story

> The underlying nature of veridical perception is brute contact between mind and truth. This guarantees rational efficacy. No state could be such contact and not be so efficacious. No state could be brute contact between mind and truth and not be reason to believe and act. After all, facts which *make true* those beliefs most directly warranted by veridical perception, and facts which *make apt* those actions most directly warranted by veridical perception, are immediately accessible *parts* of warranting experience. For example: veridically perceiving water rationalizes belief that there is water since the fact which makes this belief true is an immediately accessible part of the experience upon which the belief is rationally based. Or again: veridically perceiving water (plus thirst) rationalizes reaching out since the fact which makes that action apt is an immediately accessible part of the experience from which it aptly springs.

By collapsing the immediately accessible and the objective, Disjunctivism promises an explanation of rational efficacy which satisfies both internalists, externalists and common sense. This strikes me as the view's most attractive feature.

Having said that, the view is unable to account for delusive Rational efficacy. For the only resource left to explain this Feature is Indistinguishability. Yet the attempt to do so fails. Return once more to Macbeth. Suppose he has no reason to suspect he's suffering an hallucination. Now think of an Indistinguishability-based explanation of Rational efficacy. The story would say:

(A)   Macbeth's hallucination *prima-facie* warrants (e.g.) belief that there's a dagger before him

because

(B)   it's Indistinguishable from a veridical perception as of a dagger before him which so warrants such belief.

Appearances to the contrary notwithstanding, this account of hallucinatory Rational efficacy doesn't work. In no interesting sense of explanation does the (B)-to-(A) story merit the label. What would it so much as be for

Macbeth's warrant to spring from his inability to detect the difference between hallucinatory experience and phenomenally distinct veridical and illusory experience? Remember, that's all Indistinguishability comes to. How
then could Macbeth enjoy warranting experience merely because he cannot
introspect the genuine phenomenal difference between his experience and
veridical and/or illusory experience?

I say he could not. The mere fact that an agent cannot introspect the
difference between two experiences, one of which confers warrant via its
underlying metaphysics, does not mean the other confers warrant as well.
Rational efficacy is not closed under Indistinguishability. The latter cannot
explain the former.

This is not to say, of course, that other aspects of Macbeth's hallucination couldn't be used to do so. It might be said Macbeth's hallucination
warrants belief in a dagger before him because that hallucination makes it
for Macbeth as if a dagger is directly before him. The Rational efficacy of
Macbeth's hallucination might be explained by its Scene-Immediacy. That's
both true and consistent with Disjunctivism. But the view explains neither
Scene-Immediacy nor (therefore) Rational efficacy in Macbeth's case. When
it comes to explaining such efficacy, then, there are two cases to consider:
veridical and delusive experience. Concerning the former, Disjunctivism has
the most broadly appealing story I know. Concerning the latter, it has no
decent story at all.

Behavioural Equivalence

Disjunctivism can use Indistinguishability to explain this Feature. And it
can do so in several ways. Consider two:

(1)   Disjunctivism might say veridical perception, illusion and
        hallucination drive belief and action in parallel because they
        share a common power. The idea would be that 'look iden-
        tical' visual experiences drive belief and action in parallel
        because they share the capacity to register introspectively
        as having a certain phenomenal property. Perhaps this
        shared capacity explains more general function such as
        Behavioural Equivalence.

(2)   Disjunctivism might say veridical perception drives belief and
        action in virtue of Scene-Immediacy. It might then claim
        delusive experience follows suit via Indistinguishability.

These are empirical stories. There's no apriori reason to disbelieve them.
They conflict, though, with the common-sense explanation of Behaviour
Equivalence. It says veridical perception, illusion and hallucination drive
belief and action in virtue of Scene-Immediacy. Since they are equivalent in

Table 1.1

Disjunctive Quietism		Result
Indistinguishability	×	Takes IND for granted
Scene-Immediacy	×	Explains SI of VP. Does not explain that of I or H
Subjectivity	×	Explains S of VP and I. Does not explain that of H
Rational ≈	×	Explains R efficacy of VP. Does not explain that of I or H
Behavioural ≈	×	Explains B ≈ only by side-stepping the common-sense appeal to SI

such Immediacy, they drive belief and action in parallel. Behavioural Equivalence falls out of Scene-Immediacy plus the thought such Immediacy is the driving force behind look-based belief and action. I've argued, however, Disjunctivism fails to account for delusive Scene-Immediacy. I conclude it cannot underwrite the common-sense explanation of Behavioural Equivalence. See Table 1.1.

Disjunctivism takes Indistinguishability for granted, mishandles delusive Scene-Immediacy, Subjectivity and Rational Equivalence, and deals with Behavioural Equivalence contra common sense. Time and again the bother springs from one source. The view sets Indistinguishability work it cannot perform. It tries to squeeze visual phenomenology from Indistinguishability. But the task is hopeless. Visual consciousness cannot be got from introspective incapacity.

Even if it could, however, that would be little succour. For Indistinguishability is a datum agreed by all sides. Were it capable of explaining delusive Scene-Immediacy, Subjectivity and Rational efficacy, therefore, the explanations would be public property. A view which explains Indistinguishability would thereby yield *deeper* Indistinguishability-based explanations than Disjunctivism. So even if Indistinguishability could be used (per impossible) to explain delusive Scene-Immediacy, Subjectivity and Rational efficacy, an approach which explains Indistinguishability would trump Disjunctivism. This is yet another reason to pursue a common-factor approach to visual experience.

Now, a Disjunctivist might reject my starting assumptions. She might claim veridical perception, illusion and hallucination are not all Scene-Immediate, not all Subjective, not all Rationally efficacious. But this is drastically at odds with common sense. Delusive experience is Scene-Immediate, Subjective and Rationally efficacious. To deny this is to push oneself beyond the bounds of credulity. It's to pay too high a price for one's theory of visual experience.

People claim what it's like veridically to perceive a bent stick is the same as what it's like to suffer an Indistinguishable illusion as of a bent stick. And they claim what *that's* like is the same as what it's like to suffer an Indistinguishable hallucination as of a bent stick. People equate what it's like across veridical perception, illusion and hallucination. If that's not affirming – in non-technical language – that such experiences are phenomenally type-identical, then I don't know what would be. People do so affirm. They don't use jargon to do so. But they get the idea across. Disjunctivism rejects that from the start. It requires a shocking and unacceptable departure from the common-sense take on phenomenology.

1.4 A space of common-factor views

Faced with the choice in Figure 1.1 we should strongly incline to the left. But then we face

> *Question 2*: Is the common factor built from objects present *in* experience, or features had *by* experience?

In Figure 1.2 we see our first common-factor view: Sense-Data Theory. It consists in three claims:

(1)   Veridical perception, illusion and hallucination are relations of brute acquaintance between percipient, object and object-feature.

(2)   The objects of brute acquaintance are private.

(3)   Instances of brute acquaintance are phenomenally typed by their feature-instance *relata*.

According to this position: veridical perception, illusion and hallucination consist in brute contact between mind, object and feature. Sense-Data Theory treats all visual experience on a frame like that used by Disjunctivism in the veridical case. Sense-Data theory deploys special objects across veridical perception, illusion and hallucination. These objects, Sense Data, are off

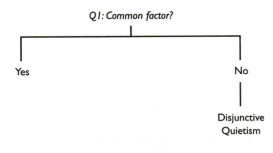

Figure 1.1

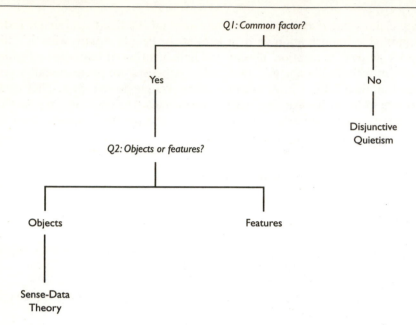

Figure 1.2

limits to public view. They show their face to a single percipient. They're neither the public objects with which we began, nor publicly scrutable parts thereof. Further: Sense-Data Theory phenomenally types visual experience by Sense-Data features. Two experiences are phenomenally type-identical iff the Sense Data they involve manifest identical features.

Now, suppose we opt for Features rather than Objects in response to Question 2. Then we face

Question 3:   Are the common features intentional or non-intentional?

In Figure 1.3 we see two more common-factor views: Intentional Theory and Raw-Feel Theory. They agree veridical perception, illusion and hallucination share an underlying nature. They agree that nature springs from features had by experience. They disagree about the nature of those features.

Intentional Theory says they're intentional. Veridical perception, illusion and hallucination are said to represent the world as being a certain way. They are said to enjoy correctness conditions. But those conditions are not thought to require, for their possession, the existence of objects or features characterized by them. They are non-object- and non-feature-involving. This means Intentional Theory treats visual experience differently than Disjunc-

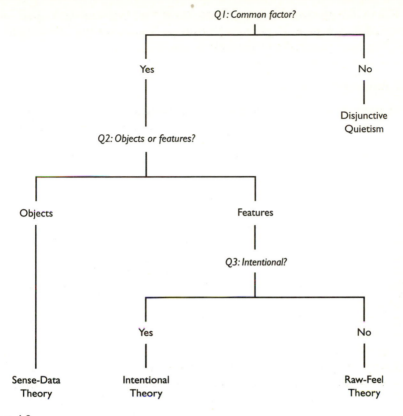

Figure 1.3

tivism treats veridical perception. Whereas the latter says worldly conditions which make such perception correct are part of the experience itself, Intentional Theory says worldly conditions which would make a given experience correct *merely individuate* the nature of that experience. Being made correct by those conditions is that experience's nature. According to this approach: veridical perception, illusion and hallucination are phenomenally typed by their intentional content. Experiences are phenomenally type-identical iff they share intentional content.

Raw-Feel Theory views the common factor via non-representational properties. These properties, Raw Feels, are definitionally tied to Subjectivity. Their possession is stipulatively why veridical perception, illusion and hallucination fall under (I1)–(I3). According to Raw-Feel Theory, that's what Subjectivity is. Moreover, the view phenomenally types experience via Raw Feels. Experiences are phenomenally type-identical iff they share Raw-Feel properties.

Figure 1.3 presents three common-factor theories. Our task is to judge how well they explain Remarkable Features. I work through them right-to-left. This leads naturally to the view I defend.

1.5 Raw-Feel Theory

Suppose veridical perception, illusion and hallucination share an underlying nature. And suppose it consists in non-representational properties definitionally tied to Subjectivity (i.e. Raw Feels). How well does this picture explain Remarkable Features? Let's see:

Indistinguishability

Raw-Feel Theory might claim its phenomenal types have veridical, illusory and hallucinatory tokens. This would ensure one could not tell, by inspecting phenomenology alone, whether a given experience is veridical, illusory or hallucinatory. Inspecting those properties would thus prove insufficient to distinguish the three types of visual experience. This looks to be an adequate explanation of Indistinguishability.

But it's not. For Indistinguishability runs on visual phenomenology. Yet Scene-Immediacy is the cornerstone of that phenomenology. It's the signal Feature of visual consciousness. There is no way to conceive visual phenomenology apart from Scene-Immediacy. What it's like to enjoy visual experience is for it to be as if objects and their features are directly before the mind. This much is non-negotiable. It implies, however, that phenomenal properties which explain Indistinguishability should also explain Scene-Immediacy. And the reason is simple: Indistinguishability springs from introspection; yet that process interrogates what visual experience is like; but Scene-Immediacy *is* what such experience is like. Hence Indistinguishable springs from Scene-Immediacy. As we're about to see, however, that spells trouble for Raw-Feel Theory. It cannot explain Scene-Immediacy. Any story it tells about Indistinguishability cuts against the bromide that Indistinguishability runs off such Immediacy.

Scene-Immediacy

Raw-Feel Theory specifies the phenomenal nature of visual experience in neither object-involving, feature-involving, nor representational terms. It does so via Subjective non-representational properties (Raw Feels). The view flatly ignores the striking object- and feature-directedness of visual experience. Yet that directedness is the hallmark of visual consciousness. For this reason, Raw-Feel Theory has no way to explain Scene-Immediacy. Nothing about Raw Feels could make their possessors Scene-Immediate. There is no hope of explanation here.

Subjectivity

Moreover, Raw-Feel Theory stipulates that Raw Feels are Subjective properties. It takes a definitional approach to the phenomenon. Hence the view cannot use its phenomenal properties to edify Subjectivity. The resulting circle would be vicious in the extreme. There's no hope of explanation here either.

Rational Equivalence

And nor can the rationality of belief and action be sensibly thought to spring from Raw Feels. Such Feels are neither object-involving, feature-involving nor representational. Nothing about them could make their possessors rationally efficacious. If Raw Feels exhaust what's common to veridical perception, illusion and hallucination, that commonality does not explain Rational Equivalence.

Behavioural Equivalence

Raw-Feel Theory looks to have a partial explanation of this Feature. It cannot explain why veridical perception, illusion and hallucination have causal powers *au debut*. But it looks to explain, provided they do, why they have equivalent causal powers. It need only ground them in Raw Feels. Since the view says such experiences share such Feels, the hypothesis they're causally relevant entails a symmetry among veridical perception, illusion and hallucination. And that looks to be kosher-though-partial explanation of Behavioural Equivalence.

But it's not. For such Equivalence runs on visual phenomenology. Yet Scene-Immediacy is integral to that phenomenology. Such Immediacy is the signal Feature of visual consciousness. It's a datum, therefore, that veridical perception, illusion and hallucination are Behaviourally Equivalent *because* they're Scene-Immediate. Since what it's like to enjoy visual experience is for it to be as if objects and their features are directly before the mind, and since what a visual experience is like helps fix belief and action it generates, veridical perception, illusion and hallucination are Behaviourally Equivalent. Any view which cannot account for Scene-Immediacy cannot explain Behavioural Equivalence. And that spells trouble for Raw-Feel Theory. It cannot deal with Scene-Immediacy. It thus cannot explain Behavioural Equivalence.

Table 1.2 shows poor results. Raw-Feel Theory mishandles every Remarkable Feature. It says nothing deep about visual experience. It postulates intrinsic properties definitially tied to Subjectivity. But that explains neither visual phenomenology nor common-sense visual function. Raw-Feel Theory is basically bankrupt.

Table 1.2

Raw-Feel Theory		Result
Indistinguishability	×	Bogus explanation
Scene-Immediacy	×	No explanation
Subjectivity	×	No explanation
Rational ≈	×	No explanation
Behavioural ≈	×	Bogus explanation

1.6 Intentional Theory

This view says veridical perception, illusion and hallucination represent the world as being a certain way. It says they have correctness conditions. But it claims those conditions do not require, for their possession, the existence of objects or features characterized by them. According to Intentional Theory: veridical perception, illusion and hallucination manifest non-object- and non-feature-involving content. How well does this picture explain Remarkable Features? Let's see:

Indistinguishability

Intentional Theory might claim its phenomenal types have veridical, illusory and hallucinatory tokens. This would ensure one could not tell, by inspecting phenomenology alone, whether a given experience is veridical, illusory or hallucinatory. Since veridical perception, illusion and hallucination share intentional phenomenal properties, inspecting those properties proves insufficient to distinguish them. This looks to be an adequate explanation of Indistinguishability.

But it's not. For Indistinguishability runs on visual phenomenology. Yet Scene-Immediacy is the cornerstone of that phenomenology. It's the signal Feature of visual consciousness. Phenomenal properties which explain Indistinguishability should also explain Scene-Immediacy. That spells trouble for Intentional Theory. For as we're about to see, the view's phenomenal properties do not fully explain Scene-Immediacy. They look relevant to the phenomenon. They don't seem to be the whole story. This means Intentional Theory looks relevant-but-insufficient to explain Indistinguishability. The view's take on Indistinguishability does not fully mesh with the bromide that it runs off Scene-Immediacy.

Scene-Immediacy

Intentional Theory encourages the idea that veridical perception, illusion and hallucination are Scene-Immediate because they're intentionally directed upon scenes. The idea is both simple and fashionable: intentional content determines that objects and features are directly before the mind. Visual experience makes it for percipients as if scenes are directly presented; and it does so because visual experience is intentionally directed upon scenes.

This is a live option. At the end of the day, however, it does not fully satisfy. Consider the difference between seeing a loved one and thinking of her. On the present view, both states are intentionally directed upon the beloved. Yet only the former is Scene-Immediate. Only visual experience *as of* the loved one is *as if* she's Immediately before consciousness. Mere thought, alas, is not like this. Scene-Immediacy looks to be a *special* kind of directedness, somehow more than intentional directedness upon a scene. In §1.8 I'll make a suggestion about this. Here I note merely that intentionality *per se* does not fully explain Scene-Immediacy. It looks relevant to the phenomenon but incapable of grounding it *tout seul*.

Subjectivity

Intentional Theory cannot explain this Feature. Think of sub-personal states or non-occurrent beliefs. They have intentionality. But there's nothing it's like to have them. Nor must you know what they're like to understand them. Nor must you have them (or something like them) to know what they're like. Intentionality looks to be one thing, Subjectivity another. Intentionality does not explain Subjectivity.

Rational Equivalence

It's natural to link rational powers with intentional content. Since Intentional Theory says counterpart veridical perceptions, illusions and hallucinations share such content, it's natural to think it implies they're rationally equivalent. Further, one might think Intentional Theory explains why such experiences have rational powers *au debut*. The idea would be that visual experience rationalizes belief and action much as belief does: via intentional content. Just as belief that snow is white rationalizes belief that something is white, visual experience representing snow's whiteness rationalizes belief that something is white. Just as belief that water is before you (plus thirst) rationalizes reaching out, visual experience representing water before you (plus thirst) rationalizes reaching out. Veridical perception, illusion and hallucination rationalize belief and action because they're intentionally directed upon scenes.

This won't do. Contrast two scenarios. In one you come to believe a cat's in the room because it looks as if there is. In the other you come to believe a cat's in the room because you fear there is. Each time you form the same belief; and you do so on the basis of states which share intentional content. If such content were all that mattered to rationality, the beliefs would be rationally equivalent. They're not. Only the visual belief has claim to rationality. Mere possession of intentionality cannot fully explain rational efficacy. It cannot be in virtue of its content alone that belief in P&Q rationalizes belief in P. It cannot be in virtue of its content alone that visual experience as if P rationalizes belief in P. Were that so, any mental state with content P would warrant belief in P (which is silly). To explain a contentful state's capacity to warrant belief in P, one must appeal to more than its content.

This does not mean intentionality is irrelevant to rational efficacy. It just means intentionality does not fully ground the phenomenon. Visual experience looks to be rationally efficacious in virtue of a *special* kind of directedness, something more than intentional directedness upon a scene. In §1.8 I'll make a suggestion about this. Here I note merely that intentionality *per se* does not fully explain rational efficacy. It looks relevant to the phenomenon but incapable of grounding it *tout seul*.

Behavioural Equivalence

Intentional Theory looks to have a partial explanation of this Feature. It cannot explain why veridical perception, illusion and hallucination have causal powers *au debut*. But it looks to explain, provided they do, why they have equivalent causal powers. It need only ground them in intentional properties. Since the view says such experiences share such properties, the hypothesis they're causally relevant entails causal symmetry among them. This looks to be kosher-though-partial explanation of Behavioural Equivalence.

But it's not. For what it's like to enjoy visual experience is for it to be as if objects and their features are directly before the mind. Yet that very phenomenology helps fix visually generated belief and action. This means any view which cannot fully account for Scene-Immediacy cannot so explain Behavioural Equivalence. As we've seen, however, Intentional Theory cannot fully account for Scene-Immediacy. It looks relevant to the phenomenon. But it does not look to be the full story. Hence Intentional theory looks relevant-but-insufficient to explain Behavioural Equivalence. See Table 1.3.

Table 1.3

Intentional Theory		Result
Indistinguishability	×	Common-factor related to IND but insufficient to explain it fully
Scene-Immediacy	?	Common-factor related to SI but insufficient to explain it fully
Subjectivity	×	No explanation
Rational ≈	?	Common-factor related to R≈ but insufficient to explain it fully
Behavioural ≈	×	Common-factor related to B≈ but insufficient to explain it fully

Intentional Theory seems relevant to Scene-Immediacy. It thereby seems relevant to other Features. Since the view cannot fully account for such Immediacy, however, it falls short of explaining them all. In §1.8 I'll suggest how it might be enriched to do better.

1.7 Sense-Data Theory

This view centres on three claims:

(1)	Veridical perception, illusion and hallucination are relations of brute acquaintance between percipient, object and object-feature.
(2)	The objects of brute acquaintance are private.
(3)	Instances of brute acquaintance are phenomenally typed by their feature-instance *relata*.

According to this position: veridical perception, illusion and hallucination consist in brute contact between mind, object and feature. Sense-Data Theory treats all visual experience on a frame like that used by Disjunctivism in the veridical case. However, the view deploys special objects across veridical perception, illusion and hallucination. These objects, Sense Data, are off limits to public view. They show their face to a single percipient. They're neither the public objects with which we began, nor publicly-scrutable parts thereof. Sense-Data Theory phenomenally types visual experience by Sense-Data features. Two experiences are phenomenally type-identical iff the Sense Data they involve manifest identical features. How well does the picture explain Remarkable Features? Let's see:

Indistinguishability

As with all common-factor views, Sense-Data Theory initially looks capable of dealing with this Feature. It might claim its phenomenal types have veridical, illusory and hallucinatory tokens. This would ensure one could not tell, by inspecting phenomenology alone, whether a given experience is veridical, illusory or hallucinatory. Since veridical perception, illusion and hallucination are said to share phenomenal properties, inspecting those properties proves insufficient to distinguish them. This looks to be an adequate explanation of Indistinguishability.

But it's not. For phenomenal properties which explain Indistinguishability must also explain Scene-Immediacy. As we're about to see, though, those of Sense-Data Theory look incapable of doing so. The view's story about Indistinguishability looks at odds with the fact that it runs off Scene-Immediacy.

Scene-Immediacy

Sense-Data Theory faces a Nasty Dilemma. It concerns the relation between Sense Data and public objects. The question is: do the former build into the latter or not?

Suppose they do. Then publicly available objects of perception are aggregates of Sense Data. The view becomes very like Disjunctivism. Just as the latter says veridical perception consists in object- and feature-involving brute contact with public objects, the former says veridical perception, illusion and hallucination consist in such contact with public-object bits. If public objects are bundles of Sense Data, after all, brute contact with the latter yields such contact with bits of the former. How well might this view explain Scene-Immediacy?

Well, both it and Disjunctivism say something non-trivial about veridical and illusory Scene-Immediacy. Disjunctivism says it's brute contact with public objects. Sense-Data Theory says it's such contact with public-object bits. If the model works for Disjunctivism – as argued in §1.3 – it should work for Sense-Data Theory as well. Unlike the former view, however, Sense-Data Theory can deal with hallucinatory Scene-Immediacy. For it claims Sense Data are the private face of public objects. This means hallucination is brute contact with an ownerless public-object face. The view can say hallucination is Scene-Immediate because it's so composed. And once more the model should work (if it works anywhere). Hence the two views offer an equally deep explanation of Scene-Immediacy. But Sense-Data Theory's explanation has greater breadth.

Yet the price we pay is high. For public objects are said to spring from private objects. They're said to build from things which show their face to a single percipient. This flies in the face of common sense. It scuppers our pretheoretic commitment to their fully public nature. It means public objects are at bottom private, that their atoms cannot be shared (as it were). And while the view is perfectly coherent, of course, it's also quite literally incredible. We should not go in for it. Our everyday commitment to fully public objects should not be sacrificed to a theory of visual experience. It should not go to secure a fingerhold on Scene-Immediacy. The price is not worth paying.

Suppose, then, Sense Data do not bundle into public objects. Suppose physical objects (and their perceptually-salient parts) are fully public. This secures common-sense metaphysics. But it threatens Scene-Immediacy. The Feature is now said to spring from brute acquaintance with private objects. And that's difficult to fathom. If objects and features immediately present in experience are truly private, then, it would seem, such experience does not place public objects immediately before the mind. This brand of Sense-Data Theory threatens to erect an opaque veil of perception. In turn that threatens Scene Immediacy.

The Dilemma springs from perennial tension between Epistemology and Metaphysics. We like access to a given domain to be maximally tight. We also like domains accessed to more than echo our nature. The trouble is having it both ways. In the present context the need is to reconcile common-sense metaphysics, Scene-Immediacy and Sense-Data Theory. I suggest a reconciling strategy in the next section.

Subjectivity

Sense-Data Theory says veridical perception, illusion and hallucination are relations of acquaintance. Common sense views acquaintance in line with (I1)–(I3). For this reason, Sense-Data Theory can say something non-trivial about the Subjectivity of visual experience. It need only appeal to our ordinary take on acquaintance plus its view that visual experience is a type of acquaintance. This is not the end of discussion, of course. But it's also not chopped liver. It proves central to the Explanatory Gap between phenomenal states and all else. That is our topic in the next chapter.

Rational Equivalence

Suppose Sense Data build into public objects. Then Sense-Data Theory is quite like Disjunctivism. The only substantive difference between them is their take on public objects. Disjunctivism says they're fully public (in line with common sense). Sense-Data Theory says they're built from private objects (contra such sense). For this reason, Sense-Data Theory can base its treatment of veridical perception's rational efficacy on that of Disjunctivism. Only minor adjustments are needed. Both say such perception puts us, near enough, in brute contact with facts. So we have:

Disjunctivism's story

> The underlying nature of veridical perception is brute contact between mind and truth. This guarantees rational efficacy. No state could be such contact and not be so efficacious. No state could be brute contact between mind and truth and not be reason to believe and act. After all, bits of facts which *make true* those beliefs most directly warranted by veridical perception, and bits of facts which *make apt* those actions most directly warranted by veridical perception, are immediately accessible *parts of* warranting experience. For example: veridically perceiving water rationalizes belief that there is water since part of the fact which makes this belief true is an immediately accessible part of the experience upon which the belief is rationally

based. Or again: veridically perceiving water (plus thirst) rationalizes reaching out since part of the fact which makes that action apt is an immediately accessible part of the experience from which it aptly springs.

By collapsing the immediately accessible and the world, Sense-Data Theory promises an explanation of veridical rational efficacy which satisfies both internalists and externalists.

But it does not satisfy common sense. For public objects are said to spring from private objects. They're said to build from things which show their face to a single percipient. As we've seen, however, this flies in the face of common sense. It scuppers our pre-theoretic commitment to fully public objects. By my lights, that commitment should not be sacrificed to a theory of visual experience. It should not go to secure a story kosher by internalist and externalist lights. The price is just too high.

Further, Sense-Data Theory is unable to account for delusive Rational efficacy. The only resource left to explain this Feature is Indistinguishability. Yet our discussion of Disjunctivism shows this won't work. When it comes to explaining Rational efficacy, then, there are two cases to consider: veridical and delusive experience. Concerning the former, Sense-Data Theory has a Disjunctivism-like story ensconced in unpalatable metaphysics. Concerning the latter, it has no decent story at all.

Suppose, then, Sense Data do not build into public objects. Suppose physical objects (and their parts) are fully public. This secures common-sense metaphysics. But it threatens Rational Equivalence. The Feature is now said to spring from brute acquaintance with private objects. And that's difficult to fathom. If objects and features immediately present in experience are truly private, then, it would seem, such experience does not rationalize thought about or action within a public domain. This brand of Sense-Data Theory threatens to erect an opaque veil of perception. That threatens Rational Equivalence. Here the need is to reconcile common-sense metaphysics, Rational Equivalence and Sense-Data Theory. I suggest a reconciling strategy in the next section.

Behaviour Equivalence

At first glance Sense-Data Theory looks to have a partial explanation of this Feature. It cannot explain why veridical perception, illusion and hallucination have causal powers *au debut*. But it looks to explain, provided they do, why they have equivalent causal powers. It need only ground them in its phenomenal properties. Since the view says they share such properties, the hypothesis they're causally relevant entails causal symmetry. This looks to be kosher-though-partial explanation of Behavioural Equivalence.

Table 1.4

Sense-Data Theory		Result
Indistinguishability	✗	Bogus explanation at best
Scene-Immediacy	✗	Plagued by the Nasty Dilemma
Subjectivity	✓	Gloss via acquaintance
Rational ≈	✗	Plagued by the Nasty Dilemma
Behavioural ≈	✗	Bogus explanation at best

But it's not. For what it's like to enjoy visual experience is for it to be as if objects and their features are directly before the mind. Yet that very phenomenology helps fix visually-generated belief and action. Any view which cannot fully account for Scene-Immediacy cannot so explain Behavioural Equivalence. As we've seen, though, Sense-Data Theory does not account for Scene-Immediacy. Its explanation of such Equivalence does not mesh with the fact that it runs off such Immediacy. See Table 1.4.

Sense-Data Theory has a line on Subjectivity. Yet it's plagued by a Nasty Dilemma. It looks capable of dealing with Scene-Immediacy – and thereby other Remarkable Features – if it builds the world from Sense Data. But this cuts against our pre-theoretic commitment to a fully public Reality. If it does not so build the world, however, it threatens a veil of perception. Either way there's bother. One thing is certain: if the view requires an essentially private metaphysics to handle Remarkable Features, it should be scrapped. The price is just too high. Luckily, it does not have to be paid.

1.8 Constructing a Theory

So far things are a mess. Disjunctivism is incomplete and unacceptably revisionary. Raw-Feel Theory edifies nothing. Intentional Theory falls short of initial promise. Sense-Data Theory is plagued by a Nasty Dilemma. See Table 1.5.

Table 1.5

	Disjunctive Quietism	Common-Factor Views		
		Raw-Feel Theory	Intentional Theory	Sense-Data Theory
Indistinguishability	✗	✗	✗	✗
Scene-Immediacy	✗	✗	?	✗
Subjectivity	✗	✗	✗	✓
Rational ≈	✗	✗	?	✗
Behavioural ≈	✗	✗	✗	✗

Having said that, bits of this Table signal real progress. The tick signals acquaintance fosters Subjectivity. The queries signal intentionality is relevant to Scene-Immediacy and Rational efficacy. After constructing it I asked myself what view (if any) would enjoy all strengths on show. And no sooner did I ask than an answer suggested itself. The combination of Intentional Theory and Sense-Data Theory would fare as well as the sum of its parts. And the queries might build into ticks when combined with the one on offer.

I decided to work it up. Eventually, the conjunction of five claims seemed best:

(1)   Veridical perception, illusion and hallucination are relations of brute acquaintance between percipient and object.

(2)   The objects of brute acquaintance are private.

(3)   The features of brute acquaintance are intentional features.

(4)   Instances of brute acquaintance are phenomenally typed by their feature-instance *relata*.

(5)   The features of brute acquaintance do not require, for their possession, the existence of objects or features characterized by them. They are non-object- and non-feature-involving.

This view combines the fecund aspect of Sense-Data Theory with that of Intentional Theory. Like the former it says visual experience consists in brute acquaintance. Like the latter it says visual experience is intentionally directed. The claims are combined by letting displays of intentionality be objects with which we're brutely acquainted. According to this approach: veridical perception, illusion and hallucination are relations of brute acquaintance between percipient and content display. These displays are private. They show their contentful face to a single percipient. I call them Intentional Tropes, and I call this view Intentional-Trope Theory.

Intentional Tropes are no part of common sense. They're theoretical entities postulated by Intentional-Trope Theory. They earn our allegiance by working for us within that theory. We must judge, therefore, how well that Theory explains Remarkable Features. Unsurprisingly, it explains everything covered by Sense-Data and Intentional Theory. But Intentional-Trope Theory does more. It handles Scene-Immediacy. And that proves the key. Let's begin, then, with the signal feature of visual phenomenology.

Scene-Immediacy

Intentional-Trope Theory says veridical perception, illusion and hallucination are intentionally directed upon physical objects and their features. It also claims they consist in brute acquaintance with the display of that intentional directedness. This, I submit, is where Scene-Immediacy comes from.

Brute acquaintance distinguishes mere intentional directedness from Scene-Immediacy. The phenomenology of the latter springs from such acquaintance with the former. Visual experiences are Scene-Immediate because they consist in brute acquaintance with the display of intentional directedness upon scenes. When there's something it's like for you to be intentionally directed upon a scene, and that what-it's-like fact is due to object-involving acquaintance with an Intentional Trope, *that's* when it is for you as if a scene is directly before the mind. Scene-Immediacy springs from acquaintance with intentional directedness.

Question: does this really work?

Answer: that depends on whether being acquainted with the display of intentional directedness is just like Scene-Immediacy. The present proposal is correct iff what it's like to enjoy brute acquaintance with the display of intentional directedness is identical to what it's like to enjoy Scene-Immediacy. So ask yourself: what *would* it be like to enjoy brute acquaintance with the display of intentional directedness?

The answer, of course, is initially unclear. The very idea of acquaintance with Intentional Tropes takes time to get used to. I had to stare hard at the view before acclimating to it. But it's often like that with new ideas. And so it is here. Reflection shows brute acquaintance with the display of intentional directedness might very well be Scene-Immediacy. The proposal is a live option. Indeed, it's the only such option to generate full-dress theory across veridical and delusive experience. My proposal, therefore, is that what it's like to enjoy brute acquaintance with the display of intentional directedness is identical to what it's like to enjoy Scene-Immediacy.

Many will object vociferously. 'Look', they'll say, 'only the equation of Scene-Immediacy and public-object-involving brute acquaintance explains visual phenomenology.' But ask yourself this: is the equation meant to be trivial or not? If so, we have no edification on offer. We have but a label for Scene-Immediacy. Yet labelling affords no purchase. No insight springs from a label.

On the other hand: if the equation of Scene-Immediacy and public-object-involving brute acquaintance is meant to be non-trivial, then we're not *guaranteed* it's true. If it's meant to be a substantive proposal about the underlying nature of veridical perception – as it should be – then our allegiance to it should be determined by how well it supports and is supported by our overall commitments.

This leaves defenders of the equation in some difficulty. For illusion and hallucination are Scene-Immediate. They're no less so than veridical perception. When a straight stick looks bent, for example, it's as if bentness is presented. Yet the equation of Scene-Immediacy with public-feature-involving brute acquaintance will not cover delusory Scene-Immediacy. Defenders of the equation face a choice: either deny illusion and hallucination *are* Scene-Immediate – thereby dropping bedrock pre-theoretic commitment – or cook up an extra view of delusion – thereby disunifying theory. If the equation of Scene-Immediacy and public-object-involving brute acquaintance is non-trivial, then, we must abandon bedrock or disunify theory. Neither option is palatable.

But suppose Scene-Immediacy is not public-feature-involving brute acquaintance. Suppose it's public-content-display-involving brute acquaintance. Then we can preserve our pre-theoretic commitment to delusive Scene-Immediacy. And we can account for it in line with veridical Scene-Immediacy. This is much more satisfying. Intentional-Trope Theory is the only view which affords a non-trivial fingerhold on the full range of visual phenomenology. For this reason, it deals gracefully with other Remarkable Features. Let's see how that goes.

Indistinguishability

Since Intentional-Trope Theory explains Scene-Immediacy, it has no trouble with Indistinguishability. It need only claim its phenomenal types have veridical, illusory and hallucinatory tokens. This ensures we cannot tell, by inspecting phenomenology alone, whether a given experience is veridical, illusory or hallucinatory. Intentional-Trope Theory says all types of visual experience have the same phenomenal nature. This means inspecting that nature will not distinguish them. The resources yield full explanation. And they do so in line with the bromide that Indistinguishability runs off Scene-Immediacy. The key is to get such Immediacy right. Common sense yields the rest of the story.

Subjectivity

Intentional-Trope Theory claims veridical perception, illusion and hallucination are relations of acquaintance. Common sense views acquaintance in line with (I1)–(I3). For this reason, the view can say something non-trivial about the Subjectivity of visual experience. It need only appeal to our ordinary take on acquaintance plus its view that such experience is a type of acquaintance. This is not the end of discussion, of course. But it's also not chopped liver. It proves central to the Explanatory Gap between phenomenal states and all else. That is our topic in Chapter 2.

Rational Equivalence

Just as it's natural to say Intentional Theory can explain this Feature, so too it's natural to say Intentional-Trope Theory can do so. And for just the same reason. It's natural to link rational powers and intentional content. Since Intentional-Trope Theory says counterpart veridical perception, illusion and hallucination share such content, it's natural to think it implies they're rationally equivalent. Further, one might think the view explains why veridical perception, illusion and hallucination have rational powers *au debut*. The idea would be that visual experience rationalizes belief and action much as belief does: via intentional content. Just as belief that snow is white rationalizes belief that something is white, visual experience representing snow's whiteness rationalizes belief that something is white. Just as belief that water is before you (plus thirst) rationalizes reaching out, visual experience representing water before you (plus thirst) rationalizes reaching out. Visual experiences rationalize belief and action because they're intentionally directed upon scenes.

This won't do. Mere possession of intentionality cannot fully explain rational efficacy. It cannot be in virtue of having content alone that visual experience rationalizes belief. Were that to be so, any mental state with content would warrant belief (which is silly). To explain a mental state's capacity to warrant belief one must appeal not only to that state's content but to some further aspect of it. This is not to say, of course, that intentionality is irrelevant to rational efficacy. It's just to say intentionality does not fully ground the phenomenon. Visual experience looks to be rationally efficacious in virtue of a special kind of directedness, something more than mere intentional directedness upon a scene.

Happily, Intentional-Trope Theory says visual experience is a special kind of directedness. It's more than mere intentional directedness upon a scene. According to the view, visual experience is acquaintance with Intentional Tropes. It's object-involving contact with 'pure intentionality'. The question is whether this can be used to explain rational efficacy. And the answer is *yes* and *no*.

On the *yes* side, brute acquaintance with Intentional Tropes yields an internalist explanation of rational efficacy:

I-story

> The underlying nature of visual experience makes it Scene-Immediate. This guarantees rational efficacy. No state could be Scene-Immediate and not be so efficacious. It's bedrock that when it is for one as if a scene is manifestly before the mind, that's reason to accept it *as* one's scene. It's bedrock that when it is for one as if a desired scene is manifestly before the mind, that's reason to act *as if* it is one's scene. Rational efficacy springs from Scene-Immediacy. Intentional-Trope Theory accounts for the former by handling the latter.

On the *no* side, brute acquaintance with Intentional Tropes cannot be used to give an externalist explanation of rational efficacy. There's no guarantee such contact reliably indicates the environment, tracks the truth or satisfies any other externalist constraint. Intentional-Trope Theory says nothing that could be used to scratch the externalist itch. Its explanation of rational efficacy is internalist through and through.

This is as it should be. The sense of Rationality in play applies with equal aplomb to veridical and delusory experience. From an externalist perspective they should not be equally rational. From such a perspective, delusive experience probably shouldn't count as rational in the first place (much less as rational as veridical perception). They are not Externally equivalent. Only veridical perception brings with it an internal connection to truth. It's entirely right and proper, therefore, that our explanation of Rational efficacy is internalist.

Behaviour Equivalence

Intentional-Trope Theory cannot explain why veridical perception, illusion and hallucination have causal powers. But it explains Scene-Immediacy. It can thus deal with Behavioural Equivalence. It need only claim such Equivalence springs from acquaintance with Intentional Tropes. Since veridical perception, illusion and hallucination are said to be identical in this respect, they turn out Behaviourally Equivalent. The resources yield partial explanation. And they do so in line with the bromide that such Equivalence runs off Scene-Immediacy. The key is to get such Immediacy right. Common sense does the rest. Intentional-Trope Theory partially explains Behavioural Equivalence.

Table 1.6 looks good. Intentional-Trope Theory explains Indistinguishability, Scene-Immediacy, Subjectivity and Rational Equivalence. It partially explains Behavioural Equivalence. The only issue it fails to resolve is the ur-causal-efficacy of visual experience. Surely that's as it should be.

I close with two objections:

Objection 1

Intentional-Trope Theory suggests visual experience consists in the presentation of 'mental postcards' (a.k.a. Intentional

Table 1.6

IT-Theory		Result
Indistinguishability	✓	Grounds the explanation via Scene-Immediacy
Scene-Immediacy	✓	Explanation via acquaintance with content
Subjectivity	✓	Gloss via acquaintance
Rational ≈	✓	Grounds the internalist explanation via Scene-Immediacy
Behavioural ≈	–	Grounds a partial explanation via Scene-Immediacy

Tropes). But that means such experience rationalizes – in the first instance at least – neither belief about nor action within the world. Rather, visual experience so rationalizes belief and action concerning mental postcards.

This is a natural worry. It has bite, however, only if Intentional-Trope Theory conflicts with Scene-Immediacy. Only then will the view mesh with the idea that visual phenomenology carries some trace of Intentional Tropes. Only then could such phenomenology reveal its content-bearing entity as well as, or perhaps in place of, its content.

But the view does not conflict with Scene-Immediacy. On the contrary, it predicts visual phenomenology carries no trace of mental postcards. All there is to that phenomenology is the message delivered by Intentional Tropes. Intentional-Trope Theory underwrites the idea that visual experience rationalizes belief about and action within common-sense reality.

Objection 2

Suppose S veridically perceives O is F. Then we have

(1)   The phenomenology of S's experience is as if O and its Fness are directly presented.

The experience is Scene-Immediate. Intentional-Trope Theory says that's because

(2)   S enjoys brute contact with an Intentional Trope which represents that O is F.

And it grounds the story in a metaphysics:

(*)   S and the trope stand in an object-involving relation, R, which is unbuilt from mental ingredients.

But this is no advance! We might as well say (1) is true because

(3)   An Intentional Trope representing that O is F manifests itself to S.

Or

(4)   Such a trope appears to S.

> It's ideology which yields a sense of progress. The meta-
> physics does no work. Yet ideology is pulled from thin air.
> Only God knows where it comes from. Only God knows
> why it's deserved. Intentional-Trope Theory has no expla-
> nation of Scene-Immediacy. Appearances to the contrary
> spring from notational sleight of hand.

This is overreaction. It's not apriori Scene-Immediacy grows from object-
involving phenomena. If so, that's news. Nor is it apriori such Immediacy
is unbuilt from mental ingredients. If so, that too is news. It's unclear
(1) grows from anything like (*). Intentional-Trope Theory has non-trivial
content. It just wraps that content in notions suffused with phenomenal
connotation.

This is no blemish. There's an Explanatory Gap between phenomenal
states and all else. No story told in non-phenomenal terms can render phenomenology pellucid. No such story can explain Subjectivity. R requires
phenomenal gloss. (2) creeps on scene because something like it is needed.
Through its use Intentional-Trope Theory does two things. It tags Scene-
Immediacy with a canonical label. And it yokes non-trivial metaphysics to
its tag.

Phenomenology is deeply puzzling. Its metaphysics can do only so much.
It can take on an intuitively pleasing shape. But that's all. The Explanatory
Gap permits no more. When it comes to *visual* phenomenology, however, a
constraint is in place. Scene-Immediacy ensures public objects and their
features figure prominently. A metaphysics of visual phenomenology is
counter-intuitive to just the extent it pushes public objects and their features
off centre stage.

Think of Disjunctivism's metaphysics in the veridical case. Public objects
and their features are up front. They play a central role. The metaphysics is
thereby intuitive. Its scope, however, is unacceptable. Yet the view's *spiel*
about delusive phenomenology lacks the right shape. It turns on Indistinguishability. Public objects and their features are too far off stage. Their
role is too peripheral. Intuition falters at the idea that Scene-Immediacy
springs from Indistinguishability. And so does theory. The idea leaves us
cold. It does so because public objects and their features are too far removed from the action.

Intentional-Trope Theory does better. It proposes a single metaphysics of
visual experience. Public objects and their features play a central role. They're
not centre stage. But they're close enough to the action. The view's metaphysics is thereby intuitive. The shift from direct to intentional tie with
public objects creates a certain freedom. In turn that freedom allows the
view's metaphysics to cover veridical perception, illusion and hallucination
in one go. The trade helps unify Remarkable Features. It's a trade worth
making.

Discussion Points

1.1 Disjunctivism's role in the chapter turns on a pair of striking features. Both concern the metaphysics of visual experience:

(A)   Disjunctivism says the metaphysics of visual perception sharply differs from that of visual hallucination. The two are built from different ingredients.

(B)   Disjunctivism says the metaphysics of visual perception derives from object- and feature-involving contact between percipient, public object and public-feature; and it adds such contact does not decompose into more primitive mental ingredients (like causation plus representation). The metaphysics of visual perception, on this view, consists in mentally brute contact between percipient and material fact.

Many philosophers defend [(A) & (B)]-like views of visual experience.

Most notoriously there's John McDowell. He's pressed such a position into service for a number of years. See McDowell (1982, 1994, 1995, and 1997). His efforts belong to a tradition known stateside as 'British Disjunctivism'. Its pioneers are Hinton (1973) and Snowdon (1981). Recently Hilary Putnam has drawn inspiration from it, converting to an [(A) & (B)]-like view of his own. See his Dewey lectures in Putnam (1994). There's also an [(A) & (B)]-like view known as the Theory of Appearing. It's discussed in Chisholm (1957 and 1965), and defended in Alston (1999) and Langsam (1997).

1.2 I doubt anyone holds Raw-Feel Theory exactly. So-called Adverbialists about visual experience come close: see Aune (1991), Butchvarov (1980), Chisholm (1957), Ducasse (1942), Sellars (1975) and Tye (1984) for discussion.

1.3 Intentional Theory is currently the most popular approach to visual experience. Within the Intentionalist Camp, of course, there is division between those who employ so-called non-conceptual content and those who abhor it. Nothing in my discussion turns on the issue. So I ignore it. See Block (1990), Dretske (1995), Evans (1982), Harman (1990), Levine (1997), Martin (1998), Peacocke (1983), Searle (1983), Tye (1992 and 1995).

1.4 Sense-Data Theory saw vigorous debate in the twentieth century. Defenders include Ayer (1936, 1973), Broad (1925), Jackson (1977), Perkins (1983), Price (1950), Robinson (1994) and Russell (1912, 1914, 1918, 1927, 1948). Critics include Austin (1962), Ryle (1949) and Strawson (1979). See also Crane (1992), Martin (1998), Snowdon (1992) and Valberg (1992).

Chapter 2

Explaining Qualia

2.1 The Problem

Ask ten philosophers about consciousness. Dozens of responses are likely to follow. I thus begin with my assumptions. First, I assume conscious states enjoy Subjectivity. Second, I assume they do so by possessing phenomenal properties. But I make no assumptions about the underlying nature of those properties. To mark this, I adopt a new word for them: 'Qualia'. Those are my starting assumptions.

Three intuitions are central to our conception of Qualia:

(I1)   There is something it's like to have a given kind of Subjective experience.

(I2)   To understand the nature of a given kind of Subjective experience, one must know what it's like to have that kind of experience.

(I3)   To know what it's like to have a given kind of Subjective experience, one must have had that kind of experience (or, failing that, a similar kind of Subjective experience).

These assumptions create The Problem of Qualia. This is the search for an explanation which begins in non-Subjective terms, proceeds in logical steps, and ends with the instantiation of Qualia. It's the search for a transparent story which entails the instantiation of Subjectivity. Exactly what it might look like will become clear in §2.2. But one thing's already certain: no one knows how to solve The Problem of Qualia.

This strikes me as something of a dilemma. Our starting assumptions form a highly plausible story. They are the bedrock of our pre-theoretic take on consciousness. But the story they tell yields a Problem we seem clueless to solve. What shall we make of this?

Many commend a conditional:

(!)   If there's no solution to The Problem of Qualia, then either dualism is true or Subjectivity doesn't exist. If there's no story which begins in non-Subjective terms, proceeds in logical steps, and ends with the instantiation of Subjectivity, then either dualism or eliminativism is right.

Not so. There's a plausible position which

(1)   accepts Qualia-based experience as governed by (I1)–(I3);
(2)   entails there is no solution to The Problem of Qualia; but
(3)   fails to entail dualism.

In this chapter I construct and defend the position. I call it *The Epistemic View of Subjectivity*. To a rough first approximation: it says Subjectivity is a by-product of epistemic features which attach to our concepts. Once this is fully appreciated, a perennial aspect of the Mind–Body Problem dissolves.

Now, Qualia are properties which bestow Subjectivity on our mental lives. Their explanation is a *property explanation*. In §2.2 I examine such explanation and construct a taxonomy. This yields a sorely-needed list of options for solving The Problem of Qualia. In section §2.3 I present The Epistemic View and its relation to (I1)–(I3). In §2.4 I show The Epistemic View entails there's no solution to The Problem of Qualia. And in §2.5 I conclude with a discussion of materialism and dualism. This sets the stage for subsequent chapters.

2.2 Property explanation

Discussion of property explanation should begin by distinguishing two strategies. The first is *causal characterization*. The second is *generative explanation*.

A causal characterization tells us when an object might gain, lose or retain a given property. It also tells us what causally follows from this. Causal characterization throws light on a target property by discriminating its causal role. Generative explanation, by contrast, tells us how a target property is instantiated in an object. It throws light on a target property by detailing how it's grounded in an object. This can be done in importantly different ways.

For example, suppose we learn an object weighs fifteen stone. In wondering about its weight we might hanker for a causal story. Our question is: what caused it to weigh fifteen stone? If the weight's sufficiently startling, however, another question will be motivated: what is it about the object which *accounts* for its weight? Here we're looking for a generative story. We do not want to know what caused the object to weigh fifteen stone. We want to know what generates its weight. When we find the object is built from a trio of five-stone parts, one of which is initially hidden, we stop wondering about the weight. Our itch for a generative story has been scratched.

Two features of this explanation are noteworthy. First, it uses weight properties to explain a weight property. This is not unusual. Often the instantiation of one property is explained by that of its conceptual relatives. By showing how ions form into chargeless particles we explain charge in terms of charge. By showing how pyramids form into cubes we explain shape in terms of shape. These are *conceptually homogeneous* explanations. Their explanatory power derives, at least in part, from the fact that *explananda* and *explanantia* are conceptually of a piece. There's little conceptual daylight between the property being explained and those doing explanatory work. Hence there's no question how the latter could do that work. It's dead obvious that charge can explain charge, shape can explain shape, and so forth.

Second, our explanation of the composed object's weight ignores the target's causal role. There is no explanatory need for a causal characterization. This is not always so. Many important generative explanations rely on a target's causal role. One starts with a causal characterization and then moves to a fuller understanding via a generative story.

Here's how it works. The causal story will be a set of causal laws associated with the target. When these are thought to pin down its nature, a generative story can be constructed. But that story will differ from our previous example. To view a target as fixed by such laws, after all, is to view it as a disposition. We may see how such a target is instantiated by finding properties which realize the disposition. Yet there'll be no guarantee those properties are conceptually tied to the target. There'll be no guarantee the generative story is conceptually homogeneous.

When we explain fragility by appeal to molecular structure, or bonding by appeal to microphysics, we have *conceptually heterogeneous* generative explanation. We explain how a dispositional target is instantiated by appeal to lower-level properties. Those properties enjoy causal profiles which ensure the target's causal role is executed. Since the nature of the target is pinned down by that role, instantiation of lower-level properties ensures that of the target. This kind of generative explanation relies on a target's causal role.

In sum: causal characterization lays out a target's causal role. Generative explanation edifies a target's instantiation. When the target is causally dispositional, its generative explanation relies on its causal characterization. Otherwise not.

These scenarios can be found in science. They can also be found in common sense. There are four target categories: non-dispositions from science and common sense, and dispositions from science and common sense. Since generative explanation comes in homogeneous and heterogeneous terms, there are eight types of such explanation. Figure 2.1 illustrates the full range. A solution to The Problem of Qualia will trace some route through this figure.

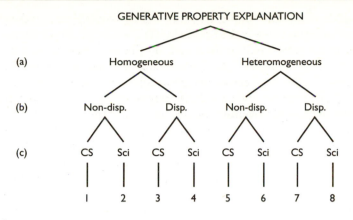

GENERATIVE PROPERTY EXPLANATION

(a) Homogeneous   Heteromogeneous

(b) Non-disp.   Disp.   Non-disp.   Disp.

(c) CS   Sci   CS   Sci   CS   Sci   CS   Sci

1   2   3   4   5   6   7   8

Figure 2.1

(a) corresponds to whether *explananda* and *explanantia* are conceptually of a piece; (b) corresponds to whether target is dispositional or non-dispositional; and (c) corresponds to whether target comes from science or common sense.

Route 1 represents a common-sense non-dispositional target which admits conceptually homogeneous explanation. The explanation of shape in terms of shape is an example. Route 8 represents a scientific disposition which admits conceptually heterogeneous explanation. The explanation of bonding in terms of valence is an example. Routes 2 to 7 are similarly easy to spot.

But notice: a conceptually homogeneous explanation of *Qualia* will explain them in their own terms. For Qualia are conceptually *sui generis*. The only properties conceptually homogeneous with Qualia *are* Qualia. In the next section we'll see why that's so. Here we note merely that homogeneous explanation of Qualia mentions them in the explanation. It thereby fails to solve The Problem.

Panpsychism is like that. It slots into the homogeneous side of Figure A. The view says all objects manifest Qualia. Subjectivity of complex objects is explained by that of components, just as weight of complex objects is explained by that of components. Panpsychism implies some Subjectivity admits conceptually homogeneous explanation. But it says Subjectivity of minimally complex objects, if such there be, is not subject to explanation. This is one reason why it fails to solve The Problem. For if there are minimally complex objects, and Panpsychism is true, their Subjectivity is inexplicable. If there are no minimally complex objects, and Panpsychism is true, all Qualia admit generative explanation. But Qualia are used in such explanation. There's no getting below the phenomena. The Problem of Qualia demands heterogeneous explanation. It demands getting below Subjectivity.

Consider a famous example. David Lewis says mental states are exhausted by their common-sense causal role (Lewis 1966). He identifies them with physical states which realize their role. Lewis promotes a theory of mind tracing Route 7 of Figure 2.1. Could this be a solution to The Problem of Qualia? More generally, could any physical explanation of Qualia succeed?

Here things become difficult. Materialists are apt to find physical views of Qualia acceptable. Dualists are apt to find them unacceptable. But it's important to be clear on what bothers the dualist.

The worry

> Successful generative explanation produces a hard-to-specify clarity concerning the target. It allows us to see how the target is instantiated. When this happens each detail of the story reports a compelling fact. And together they logically add to the target's instantiation. In the case of Lewis' theory – and physical explanations of Qualia generally – the details are uncompelling. We feel a strong urge to deny Qualia are exhausted by their role in causal/predictive practice. Qualia seem non-dispositional. But the relation between Qualia and non-dispositional physical properties is opaque to reason. Yet every physical generative explanation of Qualia must forge a non-causal link between Qualia and either intrinsic physical features or physically specified dispositions. For this reason, such explanations of Qualia rest on uncompelling detail. They lack conceptual clarity which is the hallmark of successful generative explanation.

Thus we find the Explanatory Gap. To assess its import we must uncover what produces the clarity associated with successful generative explanation. Then we may look to see whether this feature is alien to physical generative explanation of Qualia, and, if so, why it is alien. To accomplish this task we must discuss the epistemology of concepts. For as we're about to see, what counts as a good generative explanation of a property depends on the concept used to conceive it.

2.3 Concepts and Qualia

We acquire warranted belief by applying our concepts on the basis of evidence. Normally the process is defeasible. The application of a concept may cease to be warranted through introduction of new evidence. Example: you walk into a well-lit room, face a red object, and undergo a visual impression. This experience is evidence there's a red object before you. By having it you have reason to believe there's a red object before you. By having it you have reason to apply your concept RED. When told the lighting is funny, however, your evidence becomes defeated. You're no longer warranted in applying RED. The epistemic connection between your experience and RED is defeasible.

But there's a *canonical* connection between them. The epistemic link is part of what makes RED the concept it is. Nothing could be RED without being warranted by such experience. As I use the term, then, a concept is canonically linked to a kind of mental state when the epistemic link between them is individuative of the concept in question.

Recall what it's like to be conscious of something red. The experience has Qualitative character. Normally we apply RED on its basis. But we also have a conception of the experience's character. Intuitively, this is our conception of what it's like to see something red. It's our conception of the Qualitative look of redness. The feature so conceived is what gives such experience its characteristic Subjectivity. To be visually conscious of something red is *like that*.

Let's use 'q-red' to denote this property of experience, and 'Q-RED' to denote our concept of it. Q-RED is one of our concepts of Qualia. Through its use we conceptualize Qualia which attend conscious experience of red objects. By deploying Q-RED we think canonically about a phenomenal property. Specifically, we so think about the phenomenal property mental states enjoy when we experience red objects.

Like RED, Q-RED displays canonical links to evidence. No concept could be Q-RED unless certain mental states warranted – in a way I shall shortly explain – the application of that very concept. Yet beware! RED is a concept canonically applied to external objects. Q-RED is not. Q-RED is a concept so applied to mental states. RED is not. Yet both RED and Q-RED are canonically linked to the *same* (range of) mental states. This is apt to confuse. We must make a sharp distinction. We must distinguish the manner of belief fixation through which RED is canonically applied from that through which Q-RED is canonically applied.

We canonically apply RED by forming beliefs about our environment on the basis of visual experience. The manner of belief fixation is visual-belief fixation. When canonically applying Q-RED, however, we're not trying to conceptualize our environment. We're trying to conceptualize our mental states. The manner of belief fixation is not visual-belief fixation. Rather, it's *introspection*.

Concepts of Qualia are canonically applied through introspection. One should avoid modelling this procedure on vision, touch or any other sense modality. There are epistemic differences between it and all other modes of belief fixation. They prove the key to Subjectivity. So let's be clear about them.

When we see or touch or smell, for example, the salient features of our evidential states are metaphysically distinct from properties seen or touched or smelt. (And by salient features of evidential states, of course, I mean features in virtue of which they *count* as evidence.) Think of applying RED on the basis of canonical visual states. Phenomenal features of those states are an evidential intermediary of redness. There is redness and the look of redness (i.e. q-redness). Appearance and reality are distinct. Or think of applying SMOOTH on the basis of canonical tactile states. Phenomenal features of those states are an evidential intermediary of smoothness. There is smoothness and the feel of smoothness (i.e. q-smoothness). Appearance and reality are distinct here as well. But whenever evidence is distinct from the reality it indicates certain defeaters are possible. Three examples:

1   If you realize your environment is bathed in red light, you will not be warranted in believing your surroundings are red. You may nevertheless fully appreciate the *look* of your surroundings. Your canonical evidence will be defeated but neither discarded nor ignored.
2   When you realize how light interacts with air and water, you will not be warranted in believing the punting pole is bent. You may nevertheless fully appreciate the *look* of the pole. Your canonical evidence will be defeated but neither discarded nor ignored.
3   When you realize – in the dark say – that your gloves prevent feeling the table properly, you will not be warranted in believing the table is smooth. You may nevertheless fully appreciate the *feel* of the table. Your canonical evidence will be defeated but neither discarded nor ignored.

When evidence and reality are linked as in these examples, the domain conceived yields an is–seems distinction. That distinction is marked by the possibility of *conservative defeaters*. These break the link between a concept and its canonical evidence. But they leave that evidence intact. Conservative defeaters place one in an epistemic situation in which two things are true. One may fully appreciate the possession of canonical evidence for the application of a concept, but remain unable to apply that concept with warrant.

Introspection disallows conservative defeaters. When introspecting our mental states, we do not take canonical evidence to be an intermediary between properties introspected and our conception of them. We take evidence *to be* properties introspected. For example: when I introspectively notice one of my mental states is q-red, my canonical evidence for this isn't some evidential intermediary between the q-redness of my mental state and my introspection-based belief about that q-redness. My evidence just *is* the q-redness of the mental state. Introspection moves directly from the phenomenon in question to our conception of it. This is why it feels immediate. This is why we enjoy unique – and seemingly privileged – access to our mental life.

Both these philosophically charged aspects of mind result from a platitude:

(*)   If an agent applies one of her concepts of Qualia on the basis of canonical evidence, the resulting belief is true.

But it's important not to overestimate (*)'s significance. Though doubtless the root of Cartesian approaches to mind and knowledge, these features of introspection are explained by an innocuous model. It says introspection is a concept-applying procedure with two features:

(1) Concepts involved are canonically applied on the basis of mental states.
(2) Concepts involved enjoy epistemic roles which preclude conservative defeaters.

Thus it is that our concepts of Qualia are unique. They are the only concepts which fail to view their canonical evidence as an evidential intermediary for properties conceived through their canonical use.

This is why the only *properties* conceptually homogeneous with Qualia are Qualia. The reason is simple. Our concepts of Qualia have unique epistemic roles. Their individuating features ensure Qualia are conceptually *sui generis*. Anything conceived through concepts like them will yield no is–seems distinction. Anything so conceived will be a domain in which appearance *is* reality. Our Subjective life forms a tapestry in which appearance and reality coincide.

What we have, then, is The Epistemic View of Subjectivity. This is not so much a theory as a meta-theory of Subjectivity. It yields no positive solution to The Problem of Qualia. But it makes clear – in the next section – why that Problem has no such solution. It dissolves rather than solves The Problem of Qualia. Before getting to that, however, we should connect The View with our starting intuitions. There were of course three:

(I1)   There is something it's like to have a given kind of Subjective experience.
(I2)   To understand the nature of a given kind of Subjective experience one must know what it's like to have that kind of experience.
(I3)   To know what it's like to have a given kind of Subjective experience one must have had that kind of experience (or, failing that, a similar kind of Subjective experience).

These intuitions are fundamental to our conception of Subjectivity. They are the bedrock of our pre-theoretic take on consciousness. But they're not all of the same type. (I1) is a first-order claim about consciousness. It directly describes conscious states. (I2) and (I3) do not do that. They do not so describe conscious states. Rather, they directly describe how we think about such states. They concern how we understand Subjectivity. In the next section, The Epistemic View will show why there can be no explanation of (I1). But The View can be used here to explain (I2) and (I3).

To know what a Subjective experience is like is to think of it through an appropriate Qualitative concept. To know what experience of redness is like, for instance, is to know it's q-red in nature. Were someone to insist you tell them explicitly what such consciousness *is* like, you would have no choice but to say it's q-red. This is no surprise. By thinking of experience through Qualitative concepts we think of it *as* Qualitative experience. Since experience is *canonically* characterized by Qualitative concepts, we place great emphasis on knowing what it's like. After all, experience is individuated in Qualitative terms when thought of as Subjective. This is why understanding the nature of Subjective experience requires knowing what it is like. This is why (I2) is true.

Qualitative concepts are canonically linked to Subjective experience. One fails to wield such concepts if one fails to have such experience. Consider a congenitally blind person who's had nothing like visual experience of red objects. He fails to understand the claim that such experience is q-red (unlike you). He's had nothing like visual experience of redness. He fails to have possessed canonical evidence in relation to which Q-RED is minted. He lacks the conceptual apparatus needed to comprehend an explicit description of what visual experience of redness is like. One must have Subjective experience if one is to know what it's like. This is why (I3) is true.

2.4 Dissolving The Problem of Qualia

Epistemic features make our concepts of Qualia unique. They also ensure The Problem of Qualia is insoluble. They ensure the Explanatory Gap cannot be closed. Here's why.

When giving a generative explanation we tell a story. We use our concepts. One is used to pick out a target property. Others are used to pick out explaining properties. The target property is conceived by a 'target concept'. Explaining properties are conceived by 'explaining concepts'. Yet we know concepts of Qualia display canonical links to evidence. This means any candidate solution to The Problem of Qualia will be a special kind of explanation. Specifically:

(✪)   The Problem of Qualia demands a conceptually heterogeneous generative explanation of properties conceived through concepts displaying canonical links to evidence.

Call these '✪-explanations'. They give rise to a crucial question: how do concepts used in them relate to a target's canonical evidence?

✪-explanations are compelling only if explaining concepts relate sensibly to a target's canonical evidence. *This* is why The Problem of Qualia is impossible to solve. There's simply no way for explaining concepts to relate sensibly to canonical evidence for Qualia. Let me state the argument here step-by-step. Then I'll buttress its premises.

(1)   Target concepts canonically linked to evidence fit into compelling heterogeneous generative explanation only when explaining concepts connect sensibly with that evidence.

(2)   Explaining concepts connect sensibly with such evidence only when it's an evidential intermediary for the target property.

(3)   Canonical evidence for Qualia is not an evidential intermediary for Qualia.

Thus,

(4)   No heterogeneous generative explanation of Qualia is compelling. No such explanation solves The Problem of Qualia.

Comment on (1)

Any heterogeneous generative explanation of a property conceived through a concept canonically linked to evidence must vindicate those canonical links. When properties conceived through explaining concepts fail to illustrate why canonical evidence signals the property conceived by the target concept, it will be unclear why, or how, they capture that very property. Explaining properties will seem irrelevant to the target's canonical evidence. But no properties which seem irrelevant to a target's *canonical* evidence can ground a pellucid story about that target.

Imagine trying to explain colours via wavelengths but failing to say how wavelengths might look colourful. The story would be hopeless. No properties can sensibly be thought to realize colour unless they can sensibly be thought to look colourful. Or imagine trying to explain solidity via atomic structure but failing to say how such structure can feel and look solid. Again the story would be hopeless. No properties can sensibly be thought to realize solidity unless they can sensibly be thought to feel and look solid. And so forth. Compelling connection between explaining properties and target property comes through canonical evidence. This is why Premise (1) is true.

Comment on (2)

✪-explanation is compelling only when the target concept's canonical evidence is an evidential intermediary for the target property. The reason is simple. Only then will there be conceptual 'room to manoeuvre' between target property and canonical evidence. Only then will it be possible to see why an *heterogeneous* explanation might work. Only then will it be possible to forge a theoretical link from explaining properties to a conceptually dissimilar target. The link will go through canonical evidence.

Suppose we define a target property via canonical evidence. Say we identify it as the property which induces that evidence in relevant circumstances. We then discover conceptually dissimilar properties induce that evidence in those circumstances. Bingo! A ❂-explanation is on offer. It's clear why conceptually dissimilar properties realize the target.

Or suppose we take the link between target and canonical evidence to be less than constitutive. Perhaps we think it contingently causal. This too creates the possibility of seeing – albeit in a weaker sense – why a conceptually heterogeneous generative explanation might work. It creates the possibility of empirically establishing that conceptually dissimilar properties are responsible for the causal link in question. This will not logically imply explaining properties realize the target. But it will empirically confirm explaining properties appear as the target canonically appears. It will empirically establish that explaining properties look, feel, taste, sound, etc., exactly as the target canonically looks, feels, tastes, sounds, etc. And this will be so despite their conceptual dissimilarity. In the event, we'd have strong reason to suppose the target is realized by conceptually dissimilar properties.

In a nutshell: when dealing with conceptually heterogeneous explanation involving a canonically linked target concept, our only hope of forging an enlightening connection between explaining properties and target property is *through* canonical evidence. This route is non-trivial, however, only when canonical evidence and target property are distinct. Conceptually heterogeneous explanation is compelling only when canonical evidence is an evidential intermediary for the target property.

Suppose the distinction between target property and canonical evidence vanishes. One can then only locate brute correlation between conceptually dissimilar properties. There is no distinction between target and canonical evidence. There's no purchase on target through that evidence. Only by distinguishing them is such purchase possible. Only by doing so can more than brute correlation be established. This is why Premise (2) is true.

Comment on (3)

Introspection disallows conservative defeaters. Canonical evidence used in it is not an evidential intermediary for properties introspected. If it were, it would be theoretically possible to possess that evidence for some reason other than the presence of Qualia. The statement asserting this would be a conservative defeater for Qualia's canonical evidence. But that's not possible. Whenever we possess canonical evidence for our concepts of Qualia, we manifest Qualia those concepts conceive. This is ensured by the epistemic role of our Qualitative concepts. This is why Premise (3) is true.

Conclusion: The Problem of Qualia is insoluble. It's impossible to explain Subjective experience in non-Subjective terms. We're blocked from a solution by the very concepts in whose terms Subjectivity is canonically conceived.

2.5 Materialism and dualism

I began by stating my wish to construct and defend a position which:

(1)   accepts Qualia-based experience as governed by (I1)–(I3);
(2)   entails there is no solution to The Problem of Qualia; but
(3)   fails to entail dualism.

Two-thirds of the task is done. We've seen how The Epistemic View accepts the fundamental intuitions concerning Qualia-based experience. And we've seen how it entails there's no solution to The Problem of Qualia. But what of the third issue? How does The Epistemic View cut relative to the materialism/dualism debate?

Most contemporary dualists *are* dualists because Subjectivity is inexplicable. The Epistemic View shows this is mistaken. The Explanatory Gap is best explained by epistemic features of our concepts. Nothing ontically funny is required. No explanation for Qualia is possible. But it doesn't follow properties captured by our Qualitative concepts are distinct from those captured by other concepts. The Epistemic View fails to entail dualism.

On the other hand, that View fails to entail materialism as well. It provides no reason to think properties captured by Qualitative concepts are identical to, or realized by, properties captured by other concepts. The Epistemic View cuts in neither direction of the materialism/dualism debate. It's an ontically neutral view.

Discussion Points

2.1 In early 1992 I began to think seriously about why no explanation of Qualia seemed possible. The view presented here was in place by Easter of that year. Just thereafter Steve Laurence put me onto Joe Levine's work. Then I ran across Brian Loar's.

Not only does Levine (1983) do a fine job of detailing the Explanatory Gap, but Loar (1990) pioneers the idea that Levine's Gap turns on concepts rather than properties. Loar's way of putting it is less epistemic than mine – see Loar (1996) for a refined and clarified version – but the central insight is his. And it's become standard among those who deny that dualism flows from the Gap. Details vary from philosopher to philosopher. But Loar's idea remains constant: the Gap springs from how we think about phenomenology rather than how it is in itself. I agree. And so do Block and Stalnaker (1999), Levine (1993 and 1998), Papineau (1993a and 1993b), and Tye (1999).

2.2 The Epistemic View of Subjectivity underwrites two thoughts:

(1) Despite the epistemic possibility that Qualia are realized by material properties, the latter do not reductively explain the former.
(2) This inexplicability is unique: no other kind of property is *that* resistant to reductive explanation.

Some accept (1) but reject (2). They say the Explanatory Gap is but the logical gap found in aposteriori necessities. That leaves out, it seems to me, the heart of things. By deploying concepts for Qualia we seem to cotton onto their *intrinsic* nature. That's why the Gap looks more ontically relevant than logical space between 'water' and 'H$_2$O', 'Venus' and 'Phosphorus', and so forth. Full-dress theory of the Gap must explain why that's so. It must explain why it looks much more ontically relevant than any other logical space between concepts. The Epistemic View does so. Loar (1996) does so as well. And the two use structurally identical strategies. It's an interesting question whether another structure could do the job. See also Block and Stalnaker (1999), Levine (1993, 1998), McGinn (1989, 1991), Papineau (1993a, 1993b), Stubenberg (1998), van Gulick (1993, 1995).

Chapter 3

Content and Warrant

3.1 A striking analogy

There are striking parallels between theories of mental content and theories of epistemic warrant. This chapter is prompted by one of them. Namely:

> Two varieties of thought experiment dominate the theory of mental content. One derives from Hilary Putnam and the other from Tyler Burge. Putnam-style thought experiments suggest content is fixed – at least in part – by the external world. Burge-style thought experiments suggest content is fixed – at least in part – by social reality. Both encourage 'two factor' approaches to content. On such an approach, content is generated by internal and external factors. The former spring from 'within the head'. The latter spring from one's social and non-social environment.
>
> Similarly, two varieties of thought experiment dominate the theory of epistemic warrant. One derives from Edmund Gettier and the other from Ernest Sosa. Gettier-style thought experiments suggest warrant is fixed – at least in part – by the external world. Sosa-style thought experiments suggest warrant is fixed – at least in part – by social reality. Both encourage 'two factor' approaches to warrant. On such an approach, warrant is generated by internal and external factors. The former spring from 'within the head'. The latter spring from one's social and non-social environment. (See the appendix.)

Despite residing within distinct branches of philosophy, two rich literatures display similar theoretical pressures, undergo similar theoretical modifications, and, in the end, relax into the same structural position.

Why is that?

I argue it's because we bring certain pre-theoretic commitments to philosophy of mind and epistemology. I expose those commitments and show

how they explain the analogy. This will demonstrate not only that theories of content and warrant are theoretically inter-dependent, but also that joint exploration of them is compulsory. The analogy points to our deepest commitments about rational mind and its place in nature. It points to a large challenge to materialism. That challenge will dominate the following chapter.

3.2 Semantic and epistemic success

We enjoy semantic success when we think of actual objects. The Fregean tradition sees this as a composite affair. We successfully denote by consciously grasping a content which determines an existing object. Semantic success is composed from a grasping relation and a determination relation. Content is that feature conscious grasp of which determines semantic success. Content semantically connects a conscious mind to the world of objects that mind inhabits.

Similarly, we enjoy epistemic success when we know about actual facts. The Cartesian tradition sees this as a composite affair. We know by consciously grasping a warrant which determines a known fact. Epistemic success is composed from a grasping relation and a determination relation. Warrant is that feature conscious grasp of which determines our epistemic success. Warrant epistemically connects a conscious mind to the world of facts that mind inhabits.

According to Figure 3.1, content and warrant are connecting features. The former connects consciousness to the world about which it thinks. The latter connects consciousness to the world about which it knows.

We should not assume, however, that the Fregean notion of grasp differs from its Cartesian counterpart solely in terms of what is grasped. Nor should we assume the Fregean notion of determination differs from its Cartesian counterpart solely in terms of what is determined. At this stage we should prescind from all detail. We should think of Figure 3.1 as a heuristic in need

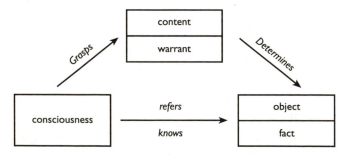

Figure 3.1

of interpretation. Our task is to flesh out its skeleton. We should ask those questions answers to which generate needed detail.

This approach has two major benefits. First, it provides a structure which guarantees we'll join issue with every major approach to content and warrant. Second, it guarantees no questions are begged along the way. Once Figure 3.1 is construed as nothing but a structure-providing heuristic, no constraints will be placed on how we flesh out its skeleton. The approach is perfectly neutral.

What, then, are the questions we must ask?

Well, consider the Figure. It suggests theories of content and warrant have three degrees of freedom. They require a story about our conscious grasp of connecting feature. They require a story about the determination of our connection to the world. And they require a story about the nature of connecting feature itself. The latter should clarify how the connecting feature in question plays the role specified by the former two stories. Figure 3.1 suggests theories of content and warrant need a story about grasp, a story about determination, and a dovetailing story about the nature of connecting feature. Examining how these might go generates a taxonomy of theories. In turn this taxonomy sheds important light on theory construction in both philosophy of mind and epistemology.

(A) Grasp

The question of grasp concerns 'distance' between connecting features and consciousness. Some theories say there's no distance. They view connecting features as part of consciousness, as proximal to consciousness. The key idea is that connecting features are essential to the nature of consciousness. Metaphorically put, content and warrant weave into the fabric of consciousness. I signal this approach by saying that content and warrant are *Transparent* aspects of consciousness. On it gross differences in them are readily introspectable. They are 'noticeable from within'.

Other theories disagree. They view connecting features as disjoint from consciousness, as distal to consciousness. The key idea is that connecting features are inessential to the nature of consciousness. Metaphorically put, content and warrant fall away from the fabric of consciousness. I signal this approach by saying that content and warrant are *Opaque* aspects of consciousness. On it gross differences in them may be 'undetectable from within'. They may leave no inner stamp on consciousness.

(B) Determination

The question of determination concerns 'distance' between connecting feature and reality. Some theories say there's no distance. They view reality as part of connecting feature, as proximal to connecting feature. The key idea is that reality is essential to the nature of the connecting feature. Metaphorically put, objects of thought weave into the fabric of content; and facts of knowledge weave into the fabric of warrant. I signal this approach by saying that content and warrant are *World-involving*. On it there can be no difference in the world side of a connected state without difference in connecting feature.

Other theories disagree. They view reality as disjoint from connecting feature, as distal to connecting feature. The key idea is that reality is inessential to the nature of connecting feature. Metaphorically put, objects of thought fall away from the fabric content; and facts of knowledge fall away from the fabric of warrant. I signal this approach by saying that content and warrant are *World-distinct*. On it there can be difference in the world side of a connected state without difference in connecting feature.

(c) Connecting feature

The question here concerns the nature of connecting feature. Some theories say connecting features are inner or private. The key idea is that connecting features are essentially 'what's given from within'. Metaphorically put, they show their face directly to their owners alone. I signal this approach by saying that connecting features are *Private*.

Other theories disagree. They say connecting features are outer or public. The key idea is that connecting features are essentially 'what's given to all'. Metaphorically put, they show their face to many at once. I signal this approach by saying that connecting features are *Public*.

Theories of content and warrant have three degrees of freedom. Within each we've distinguished two options. This yields an eight-fold partition in Table 3.1. Column A corresponds to the first degree of freedom. The query here is: what's the distance between connecting feature and consciousness? Column B corresponds to the second degree of freedom. The query here

Table 3.1

	A GRASP	B CONNECTOR	C DETERMINATION
(1)	Transparent	Private	World-involving
(2)	Transparent	Private	World-distinct
(3)	Transparent	Public	World-involving
(4)	Transparent	Public	World-distinct
(5)	Opaque	Private	World-involving
(6)	Opaque	Private	World-distinct
(7)	Opaque	Public	World-involving
(8)	Opaque	Public	World-distinct

is: what's the distance between connecting feature and reality? Column C corresponds to the third degree of freedom. The query here is: what's the nature of connecting feature itself?

Philosophers may sensibly adopt different theories of content for different types of thought. For instance, perceptually based belief might be said to involve one variety of content while theoretically driven belief involves another. Philosophers who say this will be located at different positions within Table 3.1 depending on which sort of thought is under discussion. Similarly, philosophers may sensibly adopt different theories of warrant for different routes to knowledge. For instance, perceptually based knowledge might be said to involve one variety of warrant while theoretically driven knowledge involves another. Philosophers who say this will be located at different positions within the Figure depending on which sort of knowledge is under discussion.

Having said that, every major approach to content and warrant can be found within Table 3.1. And by looking at pair-wise examples a deep connection will surface between them. In turn this will explain similarities manifested by theories in each area. It will explain why content and warrant are theoretically interdependent.

3.3 Transparent, Private and World-involving contact with the world

Suppose connecting features are Transparent, Private and World-involving. What would such a view look like? I split the question into one about content and another about warrant:

(1C) What would it mean for content to be Transparent, Private and World-involving? A clear example of this view would be any theory which claimed the mind had proximal grasp of private objects such as *Sense Data* (cf. §1.7 for a related view of visual content). The idea here is simple: thought contents are built from sensory objects and their qualities. Consider the proposition represented by an ordered pair having Sense Datum D and its quality Q as constituent elements:

(*)   <D, Q>

This proposition is said to be true at a world *w* iff D is Q at *w*. Since D is an element of (*), the proposition exists only if D does.

Now suppose when someone thinks *that D is Q* they're proximally grasping (*). Having this thought is (*) being a constitutive feature of consciousness. And (*) being such a feature of consciousness is (*)'s elements being constitutive features of consciousness. Since (*) exists only if D does, it follows someone can think *that D is Q* only if D exists. On this view, then, having such a contentful thought guarantees connection to a world. Content is Transparent, Private and World-involving.

The position enjoins unpalatable metaphysics. If this is the complete story about content, reality looks to be Private. For Sense Data are stipulatively so. If there's no more to be said about thought than this, our theory of content ensures the reality about which we think is Private *au fond*. Needless to say, this flies in the face of commonsense. And the problem obviously springs from the view that content is *both* Private and World-involving. The former commitment guarantees content is not fully public. The latter guarantees this privacy infects the world. Together they ensure we think about a domain only if it fails to be public through and through.

(1W) What would it mean for warrant to be Transparent, Private and World-involving? A clear example of this view would be any theory which grounded a factive notion of warrant in the 'inner clarity' of thought. The idea here is simple: we come to know by inspecting certain truth-marking inner qualities of thought. Warrant is generated by the recognition that our thoughts have such qualities. Since these qualities mark truth, we're guaranteed to be right by trusting them. Warrant is Transparent, Private and World-involving.

The position faces many difficulties. It's unclear thoughts have inner qualities. And it's doubtful, provided they do, that such qualities mark truth. Save divine intervention, inner qualities mark truth only if truth fails to transcend inner qualities. So once again we find an inner constraint on reality. This time, however, it springs from the view that warrant is both Private and World-involving. The former commitment guarantees warrant is not fully public. The latter commitment guarantees this privacy infects the world. Together they ensure we know a domain only if it fails to be public through and through.

Moral: There is tension within our pre-theoretic understanding of thought and knowledge. We see the mind side of the equation as consciousness-riddled. We see the world side as devoid of consciousness. By claiming aspects of the former are solely responsible for linking the two – as we find with Option (1) theories of content and warrant – we call into question the metaphysical status of the latter. By claiming Private features alone connect us to the world, we thereby call into question what sort of world we live in. Such a position forces the Public world into the Private mind.

3.4 Transparent, Public and World-involving contact with the world

Suppose connecting features are Transparent, Public and World-involving. What would such a view look like? I split the question into one about content and another about warrant:

(3C) What would it mean for content to be a Transparent, Public and World-involving? A clear example of this view would be any theory which claimed the mind had proximal grasp of *object-dependent thoughts* (cf. §1.3 for a related view of visual content). The idea here is simple: thought contents are built from external-world objects. Consider the proposition represented by an ordered pair having Bertrand Russell and the quality of having fuzzy eyebrows as constituents:

(**)   <Russell himself, the property of having fuzzy eyebrows>

This proposition is said to be true at a world *w* iff Russell has fuzzy eyebrows at *w*. Since Russell is an element of (**), the proposition exists only if Russell does.

Now suppose when someone thinks *that Russell has fuzzy eyebrows* they're proximally grasping (**). Having this thought is (**) being a constitutive feature of consciousness. And (**) being such a feature of consciousness is (**)'s elements being constitutive features of consciousness. Since (**) exists only if Russell does, it follows someone can think *that Russell has fuzzy eyebrows* only if Russell exists. On this view, then, having contentful thoughts guarantees connection to a mind-independent world. Content is Transparent, Public and World-involving.

The problem concerns interplay between the three elements. And the root worry echoes Chapter 1. Specifically, it echoes §1.3's critique of Disjunctivism. After all, mental states with (**)-like contents are Indistinguishable from mental states without (**)-like contents. Suppose you believe (**) on the basis of veridical perception. Your mental state will be Indistinguishable from one you might have enjoyed, in a Russell-free world, on the basis of hallucination. Moreover, this Indistinguishability will give rise to functional similarity. It will ensure the two prompt similar cognitive and bodily behaviour. They will drive belief and action in parallel.

As we've seen, however, when states are like this it's reasonable to expect an underlying commonality to explain the similarity. When states are Indistinguishable and thereby functionally similar it's reasonable to expect a common factor to explain their similar function. And Indistinguishability suggests the common factor is *shared content*. But that's ruled out by Option-(3) theories. To that extent, therefore, they're counter-intuitive. They're disunified and contrary to common sense. Pre-theoretically at least, the constitutive features of conscious thought are distinct from external-world objects.

(3W) What would it mean for warrant to be Transparent, Public and World-involving? A clear example of this view would be any theory which claimed the mind had proximal grasp of truths, or proximal grasp of the obtaining of truth conditions. The idea here is simple: warrant comes via proximal grasp of when external-world truth conditions obtain. This involves external-world facts forming into the fabric of consciousness. When they do, resulting beliefs are warranted and impinging facts are known. Warrant is Transparent, Public and World-involving.

Once again the problem concerns interplay between three elements. Successful recognition of facts is Indistinguishable from error. Despite such Indistinguishability, however, Option-(3) theories entail an agent is warranted in one kind of case but not the other. This confounds common sense. It makes a mockery, for instance, of the intuitive force behind sceptical doubt. Recall the sceptic's main principle:

> (S)   If an agent can't subjectively distinguish her take on one situation from that on another, she's not licensed to believe she inhabits one rather than the other.

For short: Indistinguishability enjoins warrant equivalence. This is the key sceptical thought. Sceptics use it to impugn our epistemic prospects. But we needn't endorse that use to allow there's something right about (S). In *some* good sense of 'warrant' Indistinguishability enjoins equal warrant. If that weren't so, the sceptic would have no pre-theoretic appeal. But he does. We can be sure, then, that in some sense of warrant – and perhaps even the knowledge-conferring one – Indistinguishability enjoins equal warrant. But that's precisely what Option-(3) theories deny. To that extent, therefore, they're counter-intuitive. Pre-theoretically at least, the constitutive features of conscious warrant are distinct from external-world facts.

Moral: There is tension within our pre-theoretic understanding of thought and knowledge. We see the mind side of the equation as consciousness-riddled. We see the world side as devoid of consciousness. Option (3) claims aspects of the latter constitute the former. This creates the problem of the previous section in reverse. By claiming aspects of the Public world form into the fabric of consciousness, we thereby force the Private mind into the Public world.

3.5 Transparent, Public and World-distinct contact with the world

Suppose connecting features are Transparent, Public and World-distinct. What would such a view look like? Once again it helps to split the question into one about content and another about warrant.

(4C) What would it mean for content to be Transparent, Public and World-distinct? A clear example of this view would be any theory which claimed the mind had proximal grasp of classical propositions.

A classical proposition is a fully abstract entity individuated by the mind- and language-independent truth conditions it actually has. The following gives the basic idea. Bundle objective universals into what we might call 'condition types'. Then identify *facts* with the instantiation of universals found within a bundle. And claim these bundles are the contents of thought. This amounts to identifying classical propositions with bundles of mind- and language-independent universals.

Now consider the following bundle:

(***)   <the property of being uniquely F, the property of being G>

Suppose when someone thinks *that the F is G* they proximally grasp (***). Having this thought is having (***) be a constitutive feature of conscious- ness. And having (***) be such a feature of consciousness is having (***)'s elements be constitutive features of consciousness. Content is Transparent, Public and World-distinct.

The difficulty is much the same as before. It's hard to see how anything built from mind- and language-independent entities – even universals – could become part of the fabric of consciousness. And the worry is espe- cially pressing in light of Putnam- and Burge-style thought experiments (cf. Appendix). Given *predicative* content can be modified by external-to- mind interactions seemingly extrinsic to consciousness, it's hard to believe classical propositions are the complete content of conscious thought. This generates the property-level version of the so-called 'mode of presentation problem'.

(4W) What would it mean for warrant to be Transparent, Public and World- distinct? A clear example of this view would be any theory which claimed the mind had proximal grasp of the objective reliability of our belief- forming mechanisms. According to this picture, warrant is identified with facts concerning external-world reliability which do not ensure truth. In turn these facts are woven into the fabric of consciousness. Warrant is Trans- parent, Public and World-distinct.

The problem is all too obvious. It's hard to see how anything like such reliability could be part of the fabric of consciousness. The objective reli- ability of belief-forming mechanisms is internally related to bits of reality which are no part of the fabric of consciousness. For example: such reliabil- ity is internally related to long-term frequency of true belief. They fall away from the fabric of consciousness. Anything tied intimately to them looks to do so as well. We need a story, then, to make clear how objective reliability might be Transparent. This is the warrant-theoretic analogue of the mode- of-presentation problem of (4C).

3.6 Opaque, Public and World-involving contact with the world

Suppose connecting features are Opaque, Public and World-involving. What would such a view look like? Once again we split the question into one about content and one about warrant. This time, however, we consider two views within each sub-question. The first ignores our desire to fuse connecting features with consciousness. The second respects this desire. As we'll see, the strengths and weaknesses of these theories point to a deep connection between content and warrant. This connection explains why discussion of each notion runs effortlessly in parallel. It explains why content and warrant are theoretically inter-dependent. It reveals what about that inter-dependence poses the largest challenge to materialism. That challenge will become clear in this section, stated in the next, and prosecuted in the next chapter.

(7C) What would it mean for content to be Opaque, Public and World-involving? Consider a theory which claimed thoughts enjoyed object-dependent contents solely in virtue of causal contact with the concrete elements of those contents. For instance, it might be said someone can believe Russell to have fuzzy eyebrows – where the content of this thought is given by (**) of §3.4 – only through being caused to form a belief by Russell's eyebrows. Such a view implies that having contentful thoughts guarantees semantic connection to a Public world. And since causation and object-dependent propositions are opaque to consciousness, content is Opaque, Public and World-involving.

The difficulty here is very important. The view seems to displace content from consciousness to such a degree that it cannot play one of its vital pre-theoretic roles. For content seems an intrinsic feature of conscious mental states which *explains how we reason*. It explains why we draw particular conclusions from specific evidence. The puzzle is: if content is fully disconnected from the fabric of consciousness, how can it be this driving force in thought?

Mental content generates evidential connections which *guide* thought in reasoning. Theories which claim content is fully opaque seem thereby to preclude content from this role. For when reasoning, the flow of thought seems guided by the intrinsically contentful character of our conscious mental lives *in virtue of* the evidential connections that spring from that character. Nothing extrinsic seems involved. Pre-theoretically, this is what reasoning seems to be. This is what generates a puzzle for any view of content as Opaque. (Afortiori it generates a puzzle for any view of content as Opaque, Public and World-involving.)

We might solve this puzzle by doing two things: first, finding some useful way to glue external-world contents onto the conscious features which drive reasoning; and second, avoid constructing a theory which falls into (3C). The next suggestion, familiar from the literature, does just that.

(C!) Consider the view that we have object-dependent thoughts *under a mode of presentation*. The idea is that content is a two-part invention. On the one hand, propositional content is specified via object-dependent propositions. On the other, our grasp of these propositions comes under a mode of presentation. Intuitively, modes of presentation are proximal-to-consciousness features which drive reasoning, object-dependent propositions secure our connection to the mind-independent world, and we cotton onto the latter through the former.

On this view content has a split personality. The mode-of-presentation aspect is Private. The alethic aspect is Public. Since the two are fused into one, conscious mental states enjoy semantic success vis-à-vis a mind-independent reality. What should we make of this?

Well, there's good news and bad news. The good news is simple. We have a suggestion about how object-dependent thoughts connect with consciousness. They do so under a mode of presentation. And since modes of presentation are by stipulation conscious features which drive reasoning, we may fashion a sense in which we reason as we do *because of* the content of our thoughts. For the content of thought serves-up modes of presentation. In turn these drive reasoning. In a non-trivial sense, then, we reason as we do because of the content of thought.

The bad news is also simple. We're clueless about modes of presentation. We do not know what they are, how they're woven into consciousness, how they're generated by external-world objects, how they drive reasoning. Our grip on modes of presentation is purely functional. We know what they're supposed to do. But that is all. We've no grip on what they are. We've no grip on how they manage to perform their role.

Next we consider two views of warrant. The first ignores our desire to fuse warrant with consciousness. The second does not. The strengths and weaknesses of these views reflect those found in (7C) and (C!).

(7W) What would it mean for warrant to be Opaque, Public and World-involving? Consider a theory which claims we have warrant when and because our beliefs are caused by the external-world facts which make them true. For instance, it might be said someone can believe with warrant that Russell has fuzzy eyebrows only through being caused, in the appropriate way, so to believe by the fuzziness of Russell's eyebrows. Such a view implies having warranted beliefs guarantees epistemic connection to a Public world. And since causation is opaque to consciousness, warrant is Opaque, Public and World-involving.

The difficulty with this view is directly related to the problem mentioned in (7C). Recall the relevant theory. It views content as fully opaque to consciousness. It thereby obscures the guiding role of content in thought. We're now considering a view of warrant which says that notion is fully opaque to consciousness. Does it suffer a similar fate?

Yes. But care is needed in explaining why. For suppose we echo (7C):

> Any theory of warrant which views that feature as Opaque thereby renders it too far removed from the fabric of consciousness to play the explanatory role it seems to play. For warrant explains why we reason as we do. It explains why we draw particular conclusions from specific evidence. If warrant is Opaque it's a mystery how this happens. The puzzle is: if warrant is fully disconnected from the fabric of consciousness, how can it be this driving force in thought?

Look at the second sentence. What does it mean to claim warrant explains why we reason as we do? There seems to be a kernel of truth here. But something seems dubious as well.

Consider an example. Suppose you believe Reagan was a hands-off president, and that no such president can be a good president. You conclude Reagan was not a good president. Question: why did you draw the conclusion you did? Answer: because of the warrant you had for it. But what *was* the warrant you had for the conclusion? Answer: your belief that Reagan was a hands-off president and that no such president can be a good president. Your warrant – in the presently relevant sense – amounts to no more than your other beliefs. It is their normative/evidential connection to your conclusion that is explanatory. If they hadn't had such a connection, you wouldn't have drawn your conclusion. It's because of this connection that resulting belief is warranted. Yet it would be a serious mistake to say that the latter feature – being warranted itself – explained why you drew the conclusion you did (or why you drew any conclusion at all).

On the contrary, warrant looks to be *immediately generated* by features doing the explanatory work. Warrant looks to be so generated by the evidential connections found between the content of your antecedent beliefs and your conclusion. While warrant is not itself a driving force in thought, it is immediately generated by that which is: viz., evidential connections which link contentful mental states.

This creates a puzzle for any theory which views warrant as Opaque. If warrant is fully disconnected from the fabric of consciousness, how can it be immediately generated by the evidential connections which spring from that fabric to drive thought?

We might solve this puzzle by doing two things: first, finding some useful way to glue external-world warrants onto the evidential aspects of thought;

and second, avoid constructing a theory which falls into (3W). The next suggestion, familiar from the literature, does just that.

(W!) Consider the view that warrant is a two-part invention. First, there is personal warrant. This is said to be a feature immediately generated by the evidential connections which drive conscious reasoning. Second, personal warrant is required to stand up to the facts so as to guarantee truth. When this happens we say one has 'ultimately undefeated warrant'; and this is said to convert belief into knowledge. We equate knowledge-conferring warrant with ultimately undefeated personal warrant.

Naturally, whether personal warrant is ultimately undefeated is something to which we have only distal access. Thus: personal warrant is an epistemic feature springing from the evidential aspects of thought, ultimately undefeated warrant secures our epistemic success, and we cotton onto the latter through the former.

On this view, warrant has a split personality. The personal aspect is Private. It springs from features that drive conscious reasoning. The stand-up-to-the-World aspect is Public. It springs from the interplay of Public facts. Since the two are fused into one, conscious mental states enjoy epistemic success *vis-à-vis* a mind-independent reality. What shall we make of this?

Once again there's good news and bad news. The good news is we have a suggestion about how knowledge-conferring warrant connects with consciousness. It does so when personal justification stands up to the world. The bad news is we don't know the nature of personal warrant. Nor do we understand how personal warrant is generated by the evidential aspects of thought. We have no independent purchase on the notion.

Moral: There is a deep connection between content and warrant. Each is conceptually linked to the other through its role in reasoning. This is because reasoning is a content-based, norm-guided activity – an activity which flows from the contentful aspects of our conscious mind.

Since reasoning is content based, content must drive the activity. Since reasoning is norm guided, norms must contribute as well. Yet wherever norms of evidence exist therein lie warrant-like phenomena. Warrant is immediately produced by evidential relations which spring from the content of our mental states. These evidential relations guide us in reasoning.

Here's an analogy. Suppose you find a machine hooked to the keys of a church organ. The machine monitors which notes are playing. It strikes new keys as a function of what it hears. Suppose the machine can recognize 'natural' progressions among notes. It strikes a key only if that key fits into such a progression. In the event, chords result. Harmonious sound is generated as the machine chugs along striking keys. The resulting cacophony is a note-driven activity grounded in the 'norms of harmony'. Intuitively, this is like the production of warranted belief. Our belief-forming mechanisms strike mental keys according to recognizable 'natural progressions' built from the content of our conscious mental states. When the overall system is contentfully harmonious, warranted belief results.

3.7 Conclusion

Three points can now be made with force:

(1) We bring a pair of large-scale commitments to philosophy of mind and epistemology. They are:

(A)   We're committed to a Private domain of thoughts, beliefs, desires and experiences; and we're committed to a Public domain of rocks, wind, fire, etc. The first seems riddled with consciousness. The second seems consciousness-free. Pre-theoretically: one can build the Public from the Private only by forcing the world into the mind; and one can build the Private from the Public only by forcing the mind into the world. Neither move looks kosher at first blush. This, in essence, is the take-home message from our discussion of Options (1) and (3). We're pre-theoretically committed to a dualistic ontology.

and

(B)   We're committed to the view that reasoning is a content-based, norm-guided activity that forges the link from Private to Public. Content drives mental-state transition via subsumption by norms of evidence. Warrant is the result. Pre-theoretically: Private minds connect to a Public world via a content-based, norm-guided activity: reckoning.

These are large-scale commitments. They express how we initially configure the task of building a theory of mind. Every philosophy of mind and epistemology should either coalesce with them or supply reason to give them up.

(2) We can now explain why there are deep similarities in present-day theories of content and warrant. We can also explain why there are deep similarities in the dialectical routes which have led to them. The explanation is simple. Content and warrant are joined at the hip. They're conceptually interdependent via their role in reasoning. No theoretical pressure can affect one without thereby affecting the other.

Content drives thought through norms of evidence. Warrant results from the interplay of such norms. This means if content is Janus faced – as in two-factor theories of content – then warrant will be Janus faced as well. Warrant must build from the norm-guided interplay of contentful states. On the other hand, content must be a feature possession of which renders a state subsumed by norms of evidence. This means if warrant is Janus faced – as in two-factor theories of warrant – then content will be as well. Content must be naturally policed by norms of evidence.

Thus it is that content and warrant are joined at the hip. Since each plays its proprietary role in reasoning, theories of one mirror theories of the other. Content and warrant reflect one another through a content-based, norm-guided activity.

(3) We can now explain the appeal of two-factor theories. Since our pre-theoretic ontology is dualistic, and since we suppose ourselves to think and know about the world, whatever features are responsible for this will be Janus faced. (A) and (B) – plus the idea that we successfully denote and know the world – jointly ensure two-factor structure will characterize our theories of content and warrant. Any theory which fails to manifest such structure will eventually look suspicious under scrutiny.

This explains why much of last century's philosophy of mind and epistemology have proceeded in parallel. It explains why Putnam- and Burge-style thought experiments grip in the philosophy of mind. It explains why Gettier- and Sosa-style thought experiments grip in epistemology. The availability of such a unifying explanation is itself reason to think (A) and (B) are fundamental to our conception of rational mind and its place in nature.

Having said that, (A) is a product of two things: the 'reach' of Introspection and the Explanatory Gap. Yet Chapter 2 showed the Gap springs from how our concepts work. It neither entails nor confounds dualism. By my lights, then, (A) is a natural-but-ill-grounded commitment. Its psychological and conceptual roots undermine its content.

That leaves (B). The question is whether materialism can be squared with the face of reason. Specifically, can it makes sense of the content-based, norm-guided activity which is reason? This is our next topic.

Appendix

A Putnam-style thought experiment

Suppose there is a planet, Twin Earth, that is a duplicate of Earth. But suppose the water-like stuff on Twin Earth is made from XYZ rather than H_2O. Water and Twin water are not the same thing. Now suppose Earthly Ed and his Twin-Earthly doppelganger Ted both assert 'Water is wet'. Do they express the same thought? The intuition you're invited to share is this: Ed's thought is true of water but not Twin-water; and Ted's thought is true of Twin-water but not water. Since truth conditions are determined by content, this intuition entails that factors external to Ed and Ted determine the content of their 'water' tokens. Content is fixed by the world (Putnam 1975a).

A Burge-style thought experiment

Suppose Oscar has a number of beliefs about arthritis. One is that he has it in his thigh. Oscar doesn't know arthritis is a rheumatoid ailment of the joints. Now consider Oscar's doppelganger Toscar. Oscar and Toscar are physically identical. But their linguistic communities differ. Specifically, Toscar's linguistic community applies 'arthritis' to a large range of rheumatoid ailments including the condition they both have in their thighs. Now suppose Oscar and Toscar sincerely assert 'I have arthritis in my thigh'. The intuition you're invited to share is this: Toscar speaks truly while Oscar speaks falsely. Since their thighs are physically the same, this intuition entails their utterances have distinct truth conditions. But since truth conditions are determined by content, the intuition entails that factors external to Oscar and Toscar determine the content of their 'arthritis' tokens. Content is fixed by the linguistic community to which one belongs (Burge 1979).

A Gettier-style thought experiment

Suppose I burgle your house, find two bottles of Newcastle Brown in the kitchen, drink and replace them. You remember purchasing the ale and come to believe there will be two bottles waiting for you at home. The intuition you're invited to share is this: your belief is both warranted and true. But you do not know what's going on. Knowledge-conferring warrant is fixed by the external environment (Gettier 1963).

A Sosa-style thought experiment

Suppose you are listening to the radio with colleagues. The music is interrupted. The announcer claims the President has been shot. You return to your office to work on a paper. Your colleagues continue to listen. Now the story changes. A new announcer disclaims the earlier bulletin. She labels it 'rebel propaganda'. Your colleagues don't know what to believe. But suppose the original report was reliable and true. Do you, unlike your colleagues, know the President has been shot? You believe he's been shot. They don't. But do you have knowledge they lack? The intuition you're invited to share is this: your belief is both warranted and true. But you do not know what's going on. Knowledge-conferring warrant is fixed by the epistemic community to which you belong (Sosa 1964).

Discussion Points

3.1 It's useful to see where known theories fit into Table 3.1. Russell (1912) presents a view of content that fits category (1), and Descartes (1911) presents one of warrant that does so. Evans (1982), McDowell (1986, 1994, 1997) present theories of content that fit (3), and, not surprisingly, McDowell (1982) and (1986) present one of warrant that does so. Bealer (1982), Schiffer (1987a, 1987b, 1990), Searle (1983) discuss (4)-style theories of content; and Swain (1981) defends a (4)-style theory of warrant. Millikan (1993) plumps for a (7)-style theory of content – with modes of presentation discussed extensively in Field (1977), Fodor (1987), Millikan (1997), Salmon (1986, 1989), Schiffer (1987a, 1990) – and Goldman (1967) plumps for a (7)-style theory of warrant. To my knowledge every full-dress view fits somewhere in the Figure.

3.2 Options (1), (3), (4) and (7) are discussed in the main text. Remaining options deserve comment.

Option (2): Suppose connecting features were Transparent, Private but World-distinct. Since the features determining our connection to the world are Private, the world must be *capable* of being determined by them. It's difficult to reckon how a fully objective world could be determined solely by subjective features.

Options (5) and (6): Suppose connecting features are Opaque, Private but World-involving. A feature is Opaque only if it is not part of consciousness. But a feature is Subjective only if the states that have it are conscious by having it. Nothing could be conscious by having a feature which is totally extrinsic to consciousness.

Option (8): The arguments against (8C) and (8W) mirror those against (7C) and (7W). In order to get an (8C)-theory, swap the object-dependent contents of (7C) for the classical propositions of (4C). The argument against (7C) can then be run against it. We may generate a (C!!) suffering the same fate as (C!): use classical propositions grasped under modes of presentation; then run the argument as before. To generate an (8W)-theory suffering the same fate as a (7W)-theory, collapse warrant into objective reliability; then run the argument as before. And to get a (W!!) suffering the same fate as (W!), split warrant into personal and undefeated varieties; then run the argument as before.

There is one hiccup in the otherwise perfectly symmetric situation. Note the difference between (7W)- and (8W)-theories. The former claim warrant is factive. The latter deny this. The issue turns on a question: do we need *factive* warrant to circumvent Gettier-like problems? For (independent) arguments that we do, and hence that only theories within (7W) are acceptable, see Merricks (1995), Sturgeon (1993) and Zagzebski (1996). For counter-arguments see Howard-Snyder (2000).

Chapter 4

Warrant and Reliability

4.1 Naturalism and reason

Epistemic naturalism comes in two flavours: revisionism and reductionism. Revisionists hope to recast epistemology as a non-normative branch of empirical psychology. On their view, our pre-theoretic notion of warrant will vanish from a properly reformulated epistemology. Reductionists, by contrast, hope to reduce that notion to something respectable. On their view, warrant is legitimized through its identification with naturalistic phenomena. I aim to elucidate and critique the dominant style of reductionism. It says our pre-theoretic notion of warrant reduces to probability of truth. The approach is known as *Reliabilism*.

The chapter unfolds thus: §4.2 distinguishes four types of probability. Then it explains why two of them may be used to naturalize warrant. §4.3 shows how deploying the first generates a position known as Process Reliabilism. §4.4 presents the most plausible version of this view and subjects it to scrutiny. §4.5 shows how deploying the second type of probability generates a position I call Content Reliabilism. Then it subjects the most plausible version of this view to scrutiny.

4.2 Four types of probability

It's easy to say warrant reduces to probability of truth. It's hard to effect the reduction. One reason for difficulty is clear: probability is slippery. There are many kinds of probability. We begin by distinguishing four types. Each results from the combination of two distinctions. The first concerns the objects of probability. The second concerns the metaphysics of probability.

Distinction 1

Consider a schema:

$$\text{the probability}(\varnothing) = .5.$$

Ø may be replaced by a 'that'-clause which names something true or false *in situ*. Example:

the probability(that Blair is re-elected) = .5.

But Ø may be replaced by a 'that'-clause which does not name something true or false *in situ*. Example:

the probability(that a smoker gets cancer) = .5.

When a substituend is of the first sort I call the resulting probability *alethic*. When it's of the second sort I call the resulting probability *general*. Intuitively, alethic probability is the probability a proposition is true, and general probability is the probability an arbitrary instance of a given condition-type is also an instance of another condition-type.

I mark alethic probability with lower-case letters. Expressions of the form

prob(Ø) = n

mean the alethic probability of proposition Ø being true equals n. I mark general probability with upper-case letters, and write 'G(F)' to express the general statement that an F is G. Expressions of the form

PROB[G(F)] = n

mean the general probability an F is G equals n. I remain neutral on how the probabilities relate. Specifically, I make no assumption that either reduces to the other.

Distinction 2

As we gather evidence favouring a proposition we say it becomes more probable. This signals an epistemic notion of probability. This notion is conceptually tied to that of warrant. A proposition is epistemically probable because it's supported by plenty of evidence, epistemically improbable because it's refuted by plenty of evidence, and neither because it's evidentially balanced. In contrast with epistemic probability, however, is the notion of *physical* probability. This marks a mind- and language-independent aspect of the world. Physical probability is radically non-epistemic. To a first approximation: physical alethic probability is a mind- and language-independent probability a proposition is true; and physical general probability is a mind- and language-independent probability an arbitrary instance of a given condition-type is also an instance of another condition-type. Intuitively, physical alethic probability is the stock and trade of betting shops; and physical general probability is the stock and trade of insurance companies. I follow David Lewis in calling the former *chance*, and John Pollock in calling the latter *nomic probability*.

I mark epistemic probability with *italics*. Expressions of the form

$$prob\ (\varnothing) = n$$

mean the epistemic alethic probability of $\varnothing$ being true equals n; and expressions of the form

$$PROB\ [G(F)] = n$$

mean the epistemic general probability an F is G equals n. The former is generally thought to measure rational degree of belief. The latter may be said to measure our rational disposition to accept instances of schemata, or perhaps such disposition to draw inferences with a given level of credence upon receipt of information.

I mark physical probability with **bold-face**. Expressions of the form

$$\mathbf{prob}(\varnothing) = n$$

mean the chance of $\varnothing$ being true equals n; and expressions of the form

$$\mathbf{PROB}[G(F)] = n$$

mean the nomic probability an F is G equals n.

Now, theories which reduce warrant to probability of truth mustn't traffic in epistemic probability. Such probability is conceptually tied to warrant. No reductive grip springs from collapse of warrant to epistemic probability of truth. If we're to gain such grip by collapsing warrant to probability of truth, we must collapse it to physical probability of truth. This might be done in two ways. One might reduce warrant to nomic probability of truth, or one might reduce warrant to chance of truth. The former tack yields a position known as Process Reliabilism. The latter yields a position I call Content Reliabilism.

4.3 Process Reliabilism

Consider the slogan that belief is warranted when produced by reliable means. It's readily unpacked via nomic probability. Let 'M_B' denote the belief-forming process (or mechanism) which yields belief B. Let '$T(M_B)$' express the general thought that belief produced by M_B is true. The unpacking is then

(1)   A belief B is warranted $=_{df.}$ **PROB**$[T(M_B)]$ is sufficiently high.

Here warrant is collapsed to nomic probability of truth. A means of belief production is reliable iff the nomic probability of it yielding truth is high. (1) says a belief is warranted when produced by reliable means. Intuitively, it says a belief is warranted because the nomic probability of same-sourced beliefs being true is high. Since this grounds warrant in the reliability of belief-forming processes, (1) is a variety of Process Reliabilism.

We should be dissatisfied with the view. As Goldman notes in his seminal defence of Process Reliabilism: 'A reasoning procedure cannot be expected to produce true belief if it is applied to false premises. What we need for reasoning . . . is a notion of *conditional reliability*' (Goldman 1979: 13). This suggests we distinguish belief-dependent mechanisms from belief-independent mechanisms, assess the output of the former via conditional reliability, and assess that of the latter via straight reliability.

To that end, let '$[T(M_B)/TI]$' express the general statement that belief produced by M_B is true *given* M_B receives true input. We then have the following recursive definition of warrant:

(2)   (a)   If B results from a belief-independent mechanism M_B such that **PROB**$[T(M_B)]$ is sufficiently high, then B is warranted.

(b)   If B results from a belief-dependent mechanism M_B such that **PROB**$[T(M_B)/TI]$ is sufficiently high, and M_B's input is warranted, then B is warranted.

(c)   No other belief is warranted.

Here too warrant is collapsed to nomic probability of truth. A means of belief production is reliable iff the nomic probability of it yielding truth is high. And a means of belief production is conditionally reliable iff the nomic probability of it yielding truth given it's fed truth is high. (2) says warrant is produced by reliable means and transmitted by conditionally reliable means. (2) is another variety of Process Reliabilism.

The idea behind it is simple. Perceptual belief is generated by belief-independent mechanisms. Its epistemic status turns on straight reliability. Reason-based belief is generated by belief-dependent mechanisms. Its epistemic status turns on conditional reliability. The structure is decidedly foundationalist. Perceptual belief provides the foundation. Belief-based belief builds on the foundation.

We should also be dissatisfied with (2). For

suppose that although one of S's beliefs satisfies [the antecedent of (2a) or (2b)], S has no reason to believe it does. Worse yet, suppose S has reason to believe [her] belief is caused by an unreliable process . . .

Wouldn't we deny in such circumstances that S's belief is warranted? This seems to show [(2)] is mistaken. (*ibid.*: 18)

S has salient evidence she fails to consider. Her belief is thus unwarranted. Process Reliabilism will diagnose the defect via reliability of belief-forming processes. As Goldman puts it:

(!)   the proper use of evidence will be an instance of a (conditionally) reliable process. (*ibid.*: 20)

Background defeating evidence should be used. Process Reliabilism says its proper use is the deployment of conditionally reliable mechanisms. Specifically, it's the deployment of conditionally reliable *screening mechanisms*. These prevent formation of belief defeated by background evidence.

This suggests replacing (2) with

(3)   (a)   If B results from a belief-independent mechanism M_B such that $\textbf{PROB}[T(M_B)]$ is sufficiently high, and no screening mechanism is available, then B is warranted.

(b)   If B results from a belief-dependent mechanism M_B such that $\textbf{PROB}[T(M_B)/TI]$ is sufficiently high, M_B's input is warranted, and no screening mechanism is available, then B is warranted.

(c)   No other belief is warranted.

Once again warrant is collapsed to nomic probability of truth. This time, however, reliable and/or conditionally reliable mechanisms are insufficient for warrant. (3) also requires the absence of screening mechanisms.

It should be clear a single motivation is driving theory. We are attempting to square our theory of warrant with intuition concerning the role *evidence* plays in the production of warrant. Straight nomic probability seems inadequate to the task. That explains the move from (1) to (2). Probabilities *à la* (2) seem inadequate to the task. That explains the move from (2) to (3). In each case, theoretical evolution is driven by intuition. And in each case, intuition concerns the role evidence plays in the production of warrant.

Preserving this intuition is the fundamental hurdle a non-revisionist theory must clear. If we're to capture our pre-theoretic notion of warrant, our theory must peaceably cohabit with intuition concerning evidence and warrant.

Many feel this is just where Process Reliabilism falters. Thought experiments are used to highlight the worry. They divide into two varieties. One suggests reliability is insufficient for warrant. The other suggests reliability is unnecessary for warrant. By examining each we accomplish three things. We discover the version of Process Reliabilism which does best with intuition concerning evidence and warrant. We discover why it does best. And we discover even this version does not do well enough. As we'll see: Process Reliabilism fails to naturalize our pre-theoretic notion of warrant because it fails to echo the role evidence plays in the production of warrant.

Reliability without warrant

Suppose S has a brain tumour which causes her to believe she has a brain tumour. Suppose the tumour is a highly reliable means of belief production. Question: is S's belief warranted? The target intuition is clear. We're to find it obvious S's belief is unwarranted. This is taken to show reliability is insufficient for warrant.

Unfortunately, the intuition is not widely shared. Although opponents of Process Reliabilism have it uniformly, exponents do not. And in so far as they do, it's unclear (3) conflicts with the intuition. For if S is like us she has evidence against the existence of tumours which cause beliefs made true by their source. Once this is granted, and conjoined with (!), S's belief fails to satisfy the antecedent of (3a) or (3b). Her belief is no counter-example to (3). For this reason, thought experiments like hers preach largely to the converted. They've had no serious impact in the literature.

Warrant without reliability

Suppose S is captured by evil scientists. They remove her brain and place it in a vat. The vat stimulates S in an evidence-transcendent manner. Her evidence is perfectly misleading. When she believes a cat is before her, on the basis of visual experience, her belief is sadly mistaken. Her visual mechanisms are normal-but-unreliable. Question: is her visual belief unwarranted? The target intuition is once again clear. We're to find it obvious S's belief is warranted despite the unreliability of her visual system. This is taken to show reliability is unnecessary for warrant.

The intuition has proved dialectically potent. (It's led Goldman, for instance, to abandon (3), propose a second theory, abandon it, reject the attempt to account for the intuition, and try yet once again. Goldman 1986, 1988, 1993.) But it seems to me it should not have. For if (2) handles its motivations well, a simple modification of (3) will handle demon- and vat-worlds.

Consider *why* (3) rules S's visually-based belief unwarranted. It does so by insisting its warrant be generated by straight reliability. In turn (3) so insists because vision is belief-independent. But so what? A belief needn't be based on *belief* to spring from conditionally reliable mechanisms. Think of vision. It takes visual states as input. Visual states are not beliefs. Yet they have content (as we saw in Chapter 1). Vision is perfectly subject to conditional reliability. The epistemic status of visually based beliefs, therefore, may well spring from conditional reliability.

The minimal modification of (3) induced by sceptical scenarios is a three-part invention. First, distinguish content-independent mechanisms from content-dependent ones. Second, assume perceptual states have content. And third, assess perceptual belief via conditional reliability. This yields

(3*)   (a)   If B results from a content-independent mechanism M_B such that **PROB**$[T(M_B)]$ is sufficiently high, and no screening mechanism is available, then B is warranted.

(b)   If B results from a content-dependent perceptual mechanism M_B such that **PROB**$[T(M_B)/TI]$ is sufficiently high, and no screening mechanism is available, then B is warranted.

(c)   If B results from a belief-to-belief mechanism M_B such that **PROB**$[T(M_B)/TI]$ is sufficiently high, M_B's input is warranted, and no screening mechanism is available, then B is warranted.

(d)   No other beliefs are warranted.

Two things stand out about this proposal.

First, demon worlds do not threaten it. Their denizens use experience correctly. They just happen to use misleading experience. S, for example, forms the belief that a cat is before her on the basis of it looking as if there is. This is *canonical* vision-to-belief formation. It involves believing what one sees. It leaves no scope for movement from veridical experience to false belief. The content of S's visual state trivially entails what she comes to believe on its basis. Since this is typical, however, visual belief-forming mechanisms are conditionally reliable even in demon worlds. S's visual beliefs are unreliably formed. But they're conditionally reliably formed. And since the vat ensures S's plight is evidence transcendent, she lacks evidence to impugn her experience. This means her cat belief satisfies the antecedent of (3*b). Her belief is warranted – both intuitively and *à la* (3*) – despite her brain-in-a-vat status.

Second, (3*a) is inert. It employs straight reliability. Concern with evidence leads only to conditional reliability. Witness the move from (1) to (2), the move from (2) to (3), and the adjudication of tumour- and vat-scenarios. Each time warrant springs from the interplay of evidential states (or lack thereof). Such interplay is a relation holding between *contentful* states. The probability it demands is conditional probability.

We should streamline (3*):

(4)   (a)   If B results from a content-dependent perceptual mechanism M_B such that **PROB**$[T(M_B)/TI]$ is sufficiently high, and no screening mechanism is available, then B is warranted.

(b) If B results from a belief-to-belief mechanism M_B such that **PROB**$[T(M_B)/TI]$ is sufficiently high, M_B's input is warranted, and no screening mechanism is available, then B is warranted.

(c) No other beliefs are warranted.

Once again warrant is collapsed to nomic probability of truth. This time, however, warrant is collapsed to conditional nomic probability of truth. Such probability is motivated by evolution from (1) to (4). For this reason, (4) is Process Reliabilism's theory of choice *vis-à-vis* intuition concerning evidence and warrant. And that means (4) is Process Reliabilism's theory of choice *full stop*.

This should not surprise. (!) asserts evidential force can be naturalized via reliability of belief-forming processes. In essence (4) recognizes two sources of evidential force: perceptual states and warranted beliefs. (4) is Process Reliabilism's expression of

(*) (a) If B is based on good perceptual evidence E, and the support B receives from E remains intact *vis-à-vis* background evidence, then B is warranted.

(b) If B is based on good doxastic evidence E, that evidence is warranted, and the support B receives from E remains intact *vis-à-vis* background evidence, then B is warranted.

(c) No other belief is warranted.

Process Reliabilism is driven to (4) because (*) reflects intuition concerning evidence and warrant. This reflection forces Process Reliabilism to focus on evidential interplay. In turn that forces the view to naturalize (*) via conditional reliability. (4) is the *product* of (*) and (!).

4.4 Evidential force and Process Reliabilism

Is the proper use of evidence deployment of belief-forming mechanisms with high conditional nomic probability of truth? If so, Process Reliabilism stands a good chance of naturalizing warrant. If not, it stands no chance of doing so.

I have written

(i) **PROB**$[T(M)/TI]$

to denote the conditional nomic probability used by Process Reliabilism. And I've glossed the notation by saying 'the probability of M yielding truth given true input'. This gloss can be understood in several ways. Now we must choose between them. There's no way to decide whether proper use of evidence can be cashed via Process Reliabilism without clarifying our terms.

Table 4.1

Option	x	y	$\wp(x/y)$	Type of Cond. Obj. Prob.
(a)	A	A	$\wp(A/A)$	Alethic
(b)	A	¬A	$\wp(A/¬A)$	General
(c)	¬A	A	$\wp(¬A/A)$	General
(d)	¬A	¬A	$\wp(¬A/¬A)$	General

To that end, note (i) has the form

(ii) $\wp(x/y),$

with $\wp$ a physical probability operator, x = T(M), and y = TI. Note also x and y take 'that'-clause substituends. As we've seen, such clauses work two ways within probability contexts. Sometimes they name alethic items. Sometimes they do not. (ii) has four interpretations. By letting 'A' stand for the alethic use of a 'that'-clause, and '¬ A' stand for its non-alethic use, the interpretations fall into truth-table format (see Table 4.1).

Each of these options involves conditional probability. And each involves physical probability. But (a) involves *chance*. (b)–(d) involve *nomic* probability.

To get a feel for the differences let

E   =   the proposition that 95 per cent of As are Bs and object *o* is an A;

and

C   =   the proposition that *o* is a B.

Suppose A and B are not gruesome. It follows E is strong evidence for C. Now let M be a belief-forming mechanism of S. Suppose it yields warranted belief in C on the basis of input having E as content. Question: can we naturalize the resulting warrant via conditional physical probability? We have four varieties to use (see Table 4.2).

If we're to naturalize warrant via conditional physical probability, we must do so via (a)–(d). More importantly: if we're to naturalize warrant via conditional physical probability *which attaches to belief-forming mechanisms*, we must do so via (b)–(d). Only they involve nomic probability. Only they service a notion of conditional probability suitable to ground reliability of belief-forming mechanisms. (a)-probability does not do this. **prob**(C/E) is a chance largely orthogonal to the reliability of M. The collapse of warrant to (a)-probability is considered in the next section. Right now we're talking

Table 4.2

Option	Notation	Quasi-English
(a)	**prob**(C/E)	**prob**(that o is a B/that 95% of As are Bs and o is an A)
(b)	**PROB**[C/T(I_M)]	**PROB**(that o is a B / that an M-input is true)
(c)	**PROB**[T(M)/E]	**PROB**(that an M-belief is true / that 95% of As are Bs and o is an A)
(d)	**PROB**[T(M)/T(I_M)]	**PROB**(that an M-belief is true / that an M-input is true)

about Process Reliabilism. Its success turns on whether warrant can be cashed via (b)- or (c)- or (d)-probability.

Let's consider each. Although the details become rather messy, it pays to study them. They reveal a single underlying problem for Process Reliabilism. It's the most troubling aspect of the view. (Impatient readers can skip to the Diagnosis. If it seems too quick, though, they should back up and consult the details from which it flows.)

Assume S has no defeating background evidence:

(b)-probability: Can S's belief be warranted because **PROB**[C/T(I_M)] is sufficiently high? In quasi-English: can S's belief be warranted because **PROB**(that o is a B/that an M-input is true) is sufficiently high?

No. This ignores the role evidence plays in the production of warrant. It ignores the crucial fact that S comes to believe C *on the basis of E*. (b)-probability yields a probabilistic connection between the truth of S's belief and the general fact that M is fed an *arbitrary* truth. It's insensitive to S's evidential base. For this reason, the collapse of S's warrant to (b)-probability entails:

- S is equally warranted in believing C on *any* evidential base, provided M is involved;

and

- S is *un*equally warranted in believing C on the *same* evidential base, provided an M* is involved so that **PROB**[C/T(I_M)] $\neq$ **PROB**[C/T(I_{M*})].

Both these claims are false.

To see this, let

P = the proposition that Bill and Hilary Clinton are one person;

and

M^* =   a belief-forming mechanism so that $\textbf{PROB}[C/T(I_M)] \neq \textbf{PROB}[C/T(I_{M^*})]$.

Now suppose M yields C on the basis of P, and M* yields C on the basis of E. The current proposal entails

- S's P-based M-belief in C is equally warranted to her E-based M-belief in C;

and

- S's E-based M-belief in C is unequally warranted to her E-based M*-belief in C.

This is clearly wrong. E is good evidence for C. P is no evidence for C. S's E-based M- and M*-beliefs in C are equally warranted. And her P-based and E-based M-beliefs in C are unequally warranted. (b)-probability founders on the role evidence plays in the production of warrant.

(c)-probability: Can S's belief be warranted because $\textbf{PROB}[T(M)/E]$ is sufficiently high? In quasi-English: can S's belief be warranted because $\textbf{PROB}$(that an M-belief is true/that 95 per cent of As are Bs and o is an A) is sufficiently high?

No. This too ignores the role evidence plays in the production of warrant. It ignores the crucial fact that S comes *to believe* C on the basis of E. (c)-probability yields a probabilistic connection between M yielding an *arbitrary* truth and the truth of S's evidential base. It's insensitive to a particular belief's grounding in that base. For this reason, the collapse of S's warrant to (c)-probability entails:

•• S is equally warranted in believing *anything* on the basis of E, provided M is involved;

and

•• S is *un*equally warranted in believing the *same* thing on the basis of E, provided a *M is involved so that $\textbf{PROB}[T(M)/E] \neq \textbf{PROB}[T(^*M)/E]$.

Both these claims are false.
    To see this, let

*M   =   a belief-forming mechanism so that $\textbf{PROB}[T(M)/E] \neq \textbf{PROB}[T(^*M)/E]$.

Now suppose M yields P on the basis of E, and *M yields C on the basis of E. The current proposal entails

••   S's E-based M-belief in P is equally warranted to her E-based M-belief in C;

and

••   S's E-based M-belief in C is unequally warranted to her E-based *M-belief in C.

This is clearly wrong. E is good evidence for C. E is no evidence for P. S's E-based M-beliefs in P and C are unequally warranted. And her E-based M- and *M-beliefs in C are equally warranted. (c)-probability founders on the role evidence plays in the production of warrant.

(d)-probability: Can S's belief be warranted because $\mathbf{PROB}[T(M)/T(I_M)]$ is sufficiently high? In quasi-English: can S's belief be warranted because $\mathbf{PROB}$(that an M-belief is true/that an M-input is true)?

No. This too ignores the role evidence plays in the production of warrant. And here the problem runs twice over. This suggestion suffers the infelicity of the (b)-proposal and that of the (c)-proposal. It ignores the fact that S comes to believe C *on the basis of E*, and the fact that S comes *to believe C* on the basis of E. (d)-probability yields a probabilistic connection between M yielding an *arbitrary* truth and M receiving an *arbitrary* truth. It's insensitive both to S's evidential base and to her belief's grounding in that base. For this reason, the collapse of S's warrant to (d)-probability entails:

•••   S is equally warranted in believing anything on the basis of anything, provided M is involved;

and

•••   S is *unequally* warranted in believing C on the basis of E, provided a *M* is involved so that $\mathbf{PROB}[T(M)/T(I_M)] \neq \mathbf{PROB}[T(*M*)/T(I_{*M*})]$.

Both these claims are false.
  To see this, let

J   =   the proposition that jalapeños are tastier than chillies;

and

M   =   a belief-forming mechanism so that **PROB**$[T(M)/T(I_M)] \neq$ **PROB**$[T(*M*)/T(I_{*M*})]$

Now suppose M yields J on the basis of P, and *M* yields C on the basis of E. The current proposal entails

•••   S's P-based M-belief in J is equally warranted to her E-based M-belief in C;

and

•••   S's E-based M-belief in C is unequally warranted to her E-based *M*-belief in C.

This is clearly wrong. E is good evidence for C. P is no evidence for J. S's P- and E-based M-beliefs in C are unequally warranted. And her E-based M- and *M*-beliefs in C are equally warranted. (d)-probability founders on the role evidence plays in the production of warrant.

There's a pattern here. It signals a deep-but-hitherto-unnoticed flaw in Process Reliabilism. We're now well placed to diagnose the flaw.

Diagnosis: Warrant is produced by the interplay of evidential states. Sometimes those states are beliefs. Sometimes those states are experiences. Normally, they're both. If we're to cash this with physical probability, we must do so with conditional physical probability. We must use something of the form

(ii) $\wp(x/y).$

But if we cash evidential force in Process Reliabilist terms, we must use nomic probability. This means using either (b)- or (c)- or (d)-probability.

None works. They all rely on *generalizing conditions*: (b)-probability does so in the y-slot; (c)-probability does so in the x-slot; and (d)-probability does so in both slots. This engenders good news and bad news. The good news is that it makes these probabilities suited to characterize belief-forming mechanisms. It tailors them for duty within *Process* Reliabilism. The bad news is that it guarantees the probabilistic connection they forge prescinds from local content. For nomic probability prescinds from local detail.

This explains why (b)-probability ignores S's evidential base, and why it allows that base unequal normative force on distinct occasions. It explains why (c)-probability ignores a particular belief's grounding in certain evidence, and why it disallows that evidence equal normative force on all occasions. And it explains why (d)-probability suffers all these faults. In a nutshell:

the collapse of warrant to nomic probability guarantees evidential force is *extrinsic* to content.

This is flatly counter-intuitive. E is not good evidence for C *because* a belief-forming mechanism has a physically probabilistic truth-directed property. E is good evidence for C *full stop*. The evidential force between these propositions is *intrinsic* to their content. It's determined by their nature and their nature *is* their content. Pre-theoretically, if two agents believe something on the basis of the same evidence, and have the same background information available, then they're epistemically equivalent. Either they're both warranted, both unwarranted, both rather warranted, whatever. Pre-theoretically, evidential equivalence enjoins epistemic equivalence because warrant springs from the contentful nature of content-bearing states.

Process Reliabilism misses this. Its reliability is nomic. The view prescinds from local content. It sees evidential force as extrinsic to such content. For this reason, Process Reliabilism is at odds with common sense. Since warrant is produced by the content-based norm-guided activity which is reckoning – as we saw in the last chapter – local content is crucial to it. Process Reliabilism gets that entirely wrong. Call this the Content Complaint.

4.5 Evidential force and Content Reliabilism

Reliabilism hopes to naturalize warrant via physical probability. This hope is constrained by (*). Any naturalization worth its salt must reflect the bromide that warrant springs from good evidence. If Reliabilism is to do this, it must employ conditional physical probability. Two varieties are available: general and alethic. *Process* Reliabilism chooses to the former. It thereby generates the Content Complaint. *Content* Reliabilism chooses the latter. Perhaps it fares better.

The view builds from a chance-based analysis of warrant-conferring evidence. Before approaching the topic directly – in Discussion Point 4.2 – let's work with a schema:

(Φ)   E is warrant-conferring evidence for B iff **prob**(B/E) is Φ.

And let's ignore the fact that chance evolves over time. (To prevent its chances from useless degeneracy, however, Content Reliabilism must index them to just before the earlier of E or B. This will be a theoretical echo of Hume's idea that causes are evidence for their effects and *vice versa*.) But we should be true to the lessons of §4.4. We should deploy (Φ) in a theory of this form:

(5)   (a)   If B is based on perceptual evidence E such that **prob**(B/E) is Φ, and the background evidence E* is such that **prob**(B/E&E*) remains Φ, then B is warranted.

(b)   If B is based on doxastic evidence E such that **prob(B/E)** is
Φ, that evidence is warranted, and the background evidence E* is such that **prob(B/E&E*)** remains Φ, then B is
warranted.

(c)   No other belief is warranted.

The idea here is simple: B is *prima facie* warranted when based on information the chance-connection to which renders it supported, and *ultima facie*
warranted when this goes unspoilt by background information.

Once again we see a reflection of (*). Just as (4) springs from (*) when (!)
is in play, (5) springs from (*) when (Φ) is in play. (4) and (5) reflect the
bromide that warrant springs from good evidence. They just disagree about
what *makes* evidence good. (4) sees this as a matter of nomic probability. (5)
sees it, so to say, as a matter of chance.

Now, a theory like (5) should deal with vat-worlds in line with its counterpart (4). But a problem appears once it does. Recall the vat-world challenge:

(V)   S is captured by evil scientists. They remove her brain and
place it in a vat. The vat stimulates S in an evidence transcendent manner. Her evidence is perfectly misleading.
When she believes a cat is before her, on the basis of visual
experience, her belief is always mistaken. Question: is her
visual belief unwarranted?

Not if (5) is wedded to an intentional approach to visual experience
(e.g. Intentional-Trope Theory from Chapter 1). A familiar response is then
available:

(R)   S forms the belief a cat is before her on the basis of it
looking as if there is. This is canonical vision-to-belief formation. It involves believing what one sees. It leaves no
scope for movement from veridical experience to false belief. The content of S's visual state trivially entails what she
comes to believe on its basis. According to (5), therefore,
the chance of S's belief being true given the veridicality of
her experience *is unity*. Moreover, the vat ensures S lacks
evidence to impugn her experience. So her belief is warranted – both intuitively and *à la* (5) – despite her brain-in-
a-vat status.

Now we face a problem. Visual states are essentially *defeasible*. The story
being told looks to entail their indefeasibility (in typical cases). Let *v* and *b*
be S's visual and belief states respectively. According to (R), these states say
the same thing. They both say a cat is before S. This means

$$\textbf{prob}(b \text{ is true}/v \text{ is true})$$

is a chance of the form

$$\textbf{prob}(y/y).$$

Thus, no matter what the background evidence BE:

$$\textbf{prob}[b \text{ is true}/(v \text{ is true and BE})] = 1.$$

This threatens to make v indefeasible evidence for b. The chance here is both maximal and unshiftable.

This cannot be right. Vision yields essentially defeasible evidence. Its looking to S as if a cat is before her is never conclusive reason to believe a cat is before her. This is so despite the fact that its so looking entails either a cat is before S or her visual state is non-veridical.

Here we find a puzzle *everyone* must face. It springs from two facts:

(A)   The content of experience trivially entails belief typically formed on its basis;

and

(B)   Experience is essentially defeasible.

(A) and (B) rule out a purely content-theoretic approach to defeasibility. Once experiential states are admitted into the class of evidential states, and seen to have the contents they do, defeasible interaction becomes more than a matter of content. The puzzle is to construct an approach sensitive to this fact. How shall Content Reliabilism do this?

I am not sure. But something like this seems reasonable:

(I)   Suppose mental states have content and *subscripts*. The latter indicate degree of belief, attitudinal component, etc. For example: there will be a 'b'-subscript and a 'v'-subscript. The former will mark a given state as believed, the latter will mark a given state as visually presented. When S believes $\varnothing$ she is thereby in evidential state $\varnothing_B$. When it looks to S as if $\varnothing$ she is thereby in evidential state $\varnothing_V$.

(II)   Evidential states can thus defeasibly threaten one another in distinct ways. The content of defeater may interact with that of other states to defeat one or more of them; or the content of defeater may interact with the *subscript* of other states to defeat one or more of them. The former would happen were defeater to negate the content upon which a given belief is based. The latter would happen were defeater to question the trustworthiness of states with a given subscript.

(III)   Evidential systems can thus *self-prune*. I conceive this happening when beliefs defeat evidential states in virtue of their subscript. For example, the belief that vision is untrustworthy prunes 'v'-subscripted states; the belief that hearing is untrustworthy prunes 'h'-subscripted states; and so forth. An agent's *fully pruned system* contains whatever is left once pruning has run its course. (Naturally, we'll need a chance-based analysis of pruning as well as Φ.)

The next idea is obvious: view *prima facie* warrant as in (5), and *ultima facie* warrant as fixed by chance conditional on fully pruned information. This yields

(6)   (a)   If B is based on perceptual evidence E such that **prob**(B/E) is Φ, and the fully pruned evidence E* is such that **prob**(B/E*) remains Φ, then B is warranted.

(b)   If B is based on doxastic evidence E such that **prob**(B/E) is Φ, that evidence is warranted, and the fully pruned evidence E* is such that **prob**(B/E*) remains Φ, then B is warranted.

(c)   No other belief is warranted.

Now, (6) is doubtless flawed. It's certainly underspecified. Both pruning and Φ are unfinished business. No matter: something like it is how Content Reliabilism will deal with (A) and (B). Yet any such view will sidestep the Content Complaint. For (6) reduces warrant to facts about chance. In turn those facts are a function of local content. The Content Complaint doesn't apply.

Having said that, good reckoning is more than content based. It's norm guided. Evidential force is a guiding influence on warranted thought. Evidential norms do more than describe good reckoning. They shape it. (6) misses this entirely. It grounds evidential force in chances which are a function of local content. But it forges no link from such force to the dynamics of rational thought. It says nothing about the guiding role of norms. This won't do. There's an internal link between evidential force and good reckoning. The former's essense is to guide the latter. (6) omits this. It leaves out the heart of good reasoning. Call this the Guiding Complaint.

To skirt it Content Reliabilism must use guiding norms in its analysis of warrant. This might be done in several ways. We can display their functional core, though, by adding to Stephen Schiffer's belief-box metaphor (Schiffer 1981). Here's the metaphor:

> Suppose we think in a language of thought and have functionally-defined 'boxes' in our head. There's a belief box, a desire box, a vision box, etc. To believe that P is to have a sentence which means P in one's belief box. To desire that P is to have a sentence which means P in one's desire box. To visually experience as if P is to have a sentence which means P in one's vision box.

Now think of reckoning. This entails shift in belief. (Fans of credence can alter the story accordingly.) The converse, however, is not true. Not all shift in belief is reckoning. Age, fear and beer can shift belief on their own. Yet that wouldn't be reckoning. Nor could it yield warranted belief. To produce *that* we must shift belief in proportion to, and in virtue of, evidence. Warrant springs from *norm-based* shift in belief.

So add to Schiffer's story:

> Suppose there's a *norm box* as well. Three features of it are relevant. One concerns its content, the others its function:
>
> (i) The norm box contains sentences which state evidential links between propositions. They codify one's *norms*. (I leave open whether their content is probabilistic, conditional, imperative and so forth.)
>
> (ii) A characteristic function of the norm box is to influence thought prompted by desire for truth. It has nothing to do with age- or fear- or beer-driven thought. Rather, it explains belief revision which grows from desire to believe something just if it's true. (Cf. Discussion Point 4.3.)
>
> (iii) A characteristic function of the norm box is to shape thought 'from below'. Norms influence thought 'below the conscious surface'. Their use amounts to procedural knowledge. It's the ability to shift belief in proportion to, and in virtue of, evidential force as measured by one's norms.

This yields a tinker-toy model of norm-based reckoning. It sees it as shift in the belief box, prompted by desire for truth, governed by the norm box.

The story should be kneaded into (6). And there are two spots where it must go. One is where (6) mentions basing. The other is where it mentions pruning. Norms should govern both activities. This yields

> (7) (a) If B is norm-based on perceptual evidence E such that **prob**(B/E) is Φ, and the fully norm-pruned evidence E* is such that **prob**(B/E*) remains Φ, then B is warranted.

(b)   If B is norm-based on doxastic evidence E such that **prob(B/E)** is Φ, that evidence is warranted, and the fully norm-pruned evidence E* is such that **prob(B/E*)** remains Φ, then B is warranted.

(c)   No other belief is warranted.

Here pruning goes by the norm box. Norms describe how fully pruned information is got. This is advance. Now only Φ is unfinished business.

Further, (7) sidesteps both Complaints so far canvassed. It reduces warrant to facts about chance. In turn those facts are a function of local content. The Content Complaint is inert. (7) also ensures warrant springs from evidential norms which guide rational thought. So the Guiding Complaint is too. (7) underwrites the view that warrant springs from content-based norm-guided activity. It's sensitive to much in our pre-theoretic take on rational thought. It forges an internal link between reason and content. It forges such a link between norms and the dynamics of thought.

The view is threatened, however, by another worry. Suppose E and B are logically independent empirical propositions. Suppose they satisfy your preferred chance-based analysis of warrant. (7) will then ensure S is warranted in believing B on the basis of warranted belief in E (provided no salient defeaters are lurking). But this will be entirely *contingent*. For chance is a contingent phenomenon. It will be contingent that E and B satisfy your preferred analysis. Had the world been sufficiently different – say were the chances radically altered – that analysis would judge E bad evidence for B; and (7) would judge S unwarranted in believing B on the basis of warranted belief in E. Collapse of warrant to chance ensures evidential force contingently holds between contents.

This is counter-intuitive. The evidential force between E and B is intrinsic to their content. It's fixed by their nature and that nature is their content. For this reason, E is necessarily good evidence for B. Two agents who believe B on the basis of warranted belief in E, and possess the same background information, are thereby epistemic twins. Either they're both warranted, both unwarranted, both rather warranted, etc. Common sense sees this determination of warrant by content as holding within worlds and across them. Content Reliabilism gets that wrong. It's thus at odds with common sense. Call this the Contingent Complaint.

This looks forceful. Without question it generates much anti-Reliabilist sentiment. I used to think it showed irreconcilable difference between Reliabilism and common sense. I now think it shows reconcilable difference. This will take some explaining.

To begin, note our basic grip on evidential norms is procedural. We grasp them by knowing how to engage in norm-guided thought. As with all procedural knowledge, however, one can bootstrap a more overt grip in two ways: first, by monitoring oneself during norm-governed activity; and second, by consulting intuition about imagined norm-governed activity. For instance: golfers can hit upon golf norms by monitoring themselves during play, and by consulting intuition about imagined play; speakers can hit upon linguistic norms by monitoring themselves during speech, and by consulting intuition about imagined speech; musicians can hit upon musical norms by monitoring themselves during performance, and by consulting intuition about imagined performance.

The same goes for our procedural grip on reason. We can use it to hit upon evidential norms by monitoring ourselves during thought, and by consulting intuition about imagined thought. That's what introspection and thought experiment are all about in epistemology. Our procedural grip on norms yields overt access to them via internal monitoring. For short: it yields apriori access to evidential norms.

This weakens the Contingent Complaint. And it does so in two steps. The first notes intuition about the modal status of evidential force may spring from our access to norms. The second notes such access is no mark of necessity. Both steps are credible. After all, we hit upon evidential norms in an internal way; and much we so hit upon is both necessary and taken to be so. It's more than merely possible, then, that we take evidential force to be necessary *because* it strikes us from within. Yet many contingencies so strike us. Think of mental states. They show their face via internal monitoring. They're palpably contingent. Being so given is no mark of necessity. The foundations of the Contingent Complaint are questionable. To the extent they involve our 'priviledged access' to norms, the Complaint is of dubious origin.

Yet it looked solid when stated. So what went wrong? Where did the mistake occur in the run up? Well, consider the crucial passage. Recall it spoke of logically independent empirical propositions:

(+)   Evidential force between E and B is intrinsic to their content. It's fixed by their nature and that nature is their content. For this reason, E is necessarily good evidence for B.

It's tempting to hear an argument in (+):

(#)   (1)   Evidential force between propositions is a function of their content.
     (2)   Propositions have their content essentially.
∴   (3)   Evidential force between propositions holds of necessity.

If that's the argument, however, (+) makes a hash of it. For (3) doesn't follow from (1) and (2). Just because evidential force is a function of content, it doesn't follow it's necessarily a function of content. And even if it were, it wouldn't follow it's the same function in all worlds. Not even (1)'s necessitation can join (2) to yield (3). That job requires

(4)   There's a function of content which, of necessity, measures
       evidential force between propositions via their content.

This isn't obvious. Our bootstrapped grip on norms says evidential force is
a function of content. (4) goes much further. It claims the function which
actually measures evidential force necessarily does so. That isn't clear.

Something like (4) lies behind much anti-Reliabilist sentiment. Demons
and vats make no sense in the literature without something like it in place.
Yet the principle is not obvious. Are we *really* committed to it? Or does it
overshoot the modal mark of our norms?

I say we're committed. Ordinary practice, it seems to me, supports something like (4). This can be seen by reflection on three facts. Jointly they
ensure our norms are conceptually necessary. Ironically, however, they also
undermine the Contingent Complaint. And if that's right, a great deal of
anti-Reliabilist literature has things exactly wrong.

Fact #1: When we reason about categorical matters of fact, we update our
view about how things are. The target is actuality. Our prompt might be
sensory input, conflict in belief, conflict in credence, new interest. In all
cases, though, one set of norms is in place. One set governs what happens.
It's not as if N governs resolving whether $\varnothing$ when the question is prompted
by conflict in belief, whereas N^* governs that question when prompted by
new interest. No. One set of norms governs throughout. One set governs
reasoning about actuality.

Further, use of a norm to reckon categorically reflects tacit commitment
to it measuring actual evidential relations. How we so reckon and how we
see evidence go hand in hand. Norms used in such thought are thereby
tacitly taken to be actual. This principle falls out of ordinary practice:

(P1)   Norms governing categorical thought reflect tacit commit-
            ment to evidential relations in the world.

Fact #2: When we reason about hypothetical matters of fact, we update our
view about hypothetical reality. Once again our prompt might be sensory
input, conflict in belief, conflict in credence, new interest. Here too one set
of norms is in place. One set governs what happens. It's not as if N governs
resolving whether $\varnothing$ under the supposition that $\triangle$ when the question is
prompted by conflict in belief, whereas N^* governs the conditional question
when prompted by new interest. No. One set of norms governs throughout.
One set governs suppositional reasoning.

Such reasoning has three moving parts. It involves a supposition, background assumptions relative to which it's made, and norms to guide thought
from the first relative to the second. When sure S is false, for instance, you
might wonder what would be so were S true. To answer you might reason

suppositionally from S. This will proceed relative to assumptions A_1–A_n. It will be guided by norms of thought. Conclusions so reached will inform what you take to be non-actuality. They'll reflect your take on worlds at which A_1–A_n and S are all true.

Further, there's an internal link between norms used to reckon suppositionally and those tacitly held to obtain within situations targeted by such reckoning. How we reckon about hypotheticals and how we see evidential force within them go hand in hand. Using a norm to reckon suppositionally thereby echos commitment to it measuring evidential relations within the situation about which we reckon. Norms used in such thought are tacitly taken to hold counterfactually. This principle falls out of ordinary practice:

(P2)   Norms governing suppositional thought reflect tacit commitment to evidential relations in other worlds.

Fact #3: We update our view of the world by reasoning categorically. We update our view of other worlds by reasoning suppositionally. It's of first importance to realize, however, that both kinds of reasoning are governed by one set of norms. Those at work in categorical thought govern suppositional thought. Those at work in suppositional thought govern categorical thought. $\varnothing$ is categorical evidence for $\triangle$ iff it's suppositional evidence for $\triangle$. In both cases it might be defeasible. But it indicates as it does in one context iff it so indicates in the other.

It's easy to see why this should be. Two points explain the convergence:

(a)   Suppositional reasoning fixes conditional commitment;

and

(b)   Such commitment figures in actuality-directed thought.

There's an internal link between reasoning suppositionally from A to B and believing (if A, B). Suppositional reasoning and conditional belief go hand in hand. No matter which 'if' is in play, however, it figures validly in *modus ponens* (and perhaps other inferential relations). All conditionals do that. Otherwise they don't deserve their name. Commitments fixed by suppositional thought feed into actuality-directed thought.

This explains why the same norms govern both categorical and suppositional thought. The latter leads to conditional commitment. The former uses such commitment in actuality-directed reckoning. To avoid epistemic disaster, then, norms governing each type of thought coincide. Divergence between them might lead to two bits of bother. It might license views of actuality unwarranted by actuality-targeted norms. It might license such views in conflict with those got via such norms. To avoid this, yet freely mix suppositional and categorical thought, the same norms are used through-out. They govern categorical and suppositional thought. They have global applicability. This principle falls out of ordinary practice:

(P3)   A norm governs categorical thought iff it governs supposi-tional thought.

(P1)–(P3) jointly explain why evidential norms are conceptually necessary. To see this, suppose N governs categorical thought. (P1) implies this echos commitment to N measuring evidential force in actuality. (P3) implies N governs suppositional thought. By (P2), then, we take N to measure non-actual evidential force. In this sense N is conceptually necessary. It measures actual and non-actual evidential force. Similarly, suppose N governs suppo-sitional thought. (P2) implies this echos commitment to N measuring evid-ential force in non-actuality. (P3) implies N governs categorical thought. By (P1), then, we take N to measure actual evidential force. This too means N measures actual and non-actual evidential force. Conclusion: norms are con-ceptually necessary.

Now recall the claim behind the Contingent Complaint:

(4)   There's a function of content which, of necessity, measures evidential force between propositions via their content.

By my lights, ordinary practice is committed to (4). Norms lay down a function of content (or near enough). It measures evidential force. Norms are conceptually necessary. So the measure is too. It works across concep-tual possibility.

This is the root of the Contingent Complaint. Content Reliabilism meas-ures evidential force via chance. Chance is conceptually contingent. Eviden-tial force is not. This means Content Reliabilism grossly mistakes the modal character of our norms. And that, in turn, yields the 'gut intuition' behind much anti-Reliabilist literature.

I used to think the modal mismatch here showed a deep flaw in Reliabilism. I gave anti-Reliabilist talks based on it. Time and again, immanent internalists would endorse my *spiel* as crystallizing their sentiments. But that all now strikes me as error. For one of the modalities involved in the modal mis-match is palpably procedural. True, (P1)–(P3) ensure norms hold across conceptual possibility. But that means no more than this: we can make no sense of what would be the case were our norms not to govern. In a sense we find that idea incoherent. This is true, however, for a simple reason. We can make no sense of *anything* without using our norms. Yet their use signals tacit commitment to them. For this reason, we can make no sense of what would be the case if our norms failed to bite. To suppose them away is to generate incoherence.

This does not mean our norms are objectively right. It just means we lose our way by supposing otherwise. We become muddled at the thought they are 'wrong'. Endorsing it *sans caveat* entails suspending allegiance to them, suspending their purchase upon us. That is something we cannot coherently fathom.

Ask yourself this: how would the Nicks do were our norms not to bite? Can't say? That's no surprise. God knows what to think in those circumstances. This shows nothing objective about our norms. It certainly doesn't establish an objective link between them and the Nicks. The incoherence springs from procedural necessity. We reckon by using our norms. And we do so of procedural necessity. Hence we fall mute when their bite is suspended.

What goes for the Nicks goes for everything. Afortiori it goes for the norms. We can make no sense of their being 'flat wrong'. That involves suspending their purchase upon us. We've no clue *what* to think once that's done. For we've no clue *how* to think once that's done. This doesn't mean our norms are objectively necessary. Nor does it mean they're objectively right. It shows nothing objective about them. It shows merely this: we fall mute when their bite is suspended. That's why they're conceptually necessary.

Such necessity is palpably epistemic. It springs from procedure writ into practice. This means the Contingent Complaint is bogus. For it rejects Content Reliabilism due to modal mismatch. Yet the modality it uses is procedural. The Complaint rests on a simple-but-irrelevant fact: no chance-based analysis of warrant is procedurally writ into practice. No such analysis founds our procedural grip on norms.

Big deal. Content Reliabilism doesn't aim to be writ into practice. Its goal is to state objective facts about governing procedures which *make them* warrant-conferring. It claims such procedures yield warrant because they're chance-related to truth in the right way. Whether this fact about them is writ in practice is entirely beside the point. Whether it's objectively contingent is too.

Content Reliabilism can happily admit the conceptual (and 'metaphysical') possibility that our actual norms fail to be appropriately chance-related to truth. What matters by its lights is whether they're *in fact* so related to truth. It's no part of the view that this is writ into practice. It's no part of the view that this is objectively necessary. What matters is whether the world is kind to us. What matters is whether our governing procedures cotton onto truth tightly enough in actuality.

The upshot is simple: Content Reliabilism might be right. Once it takes (7)'s form the view has much to recommend it. It forges an internal link between content and norms. It forges such a link between norms and our practice. The big question is whether Φ can be specified in pleasing fashion. The big question is whether the world is kind. And that, I take it, is very much an open issue [4.2].

Discussion Points

4.1 Process Reliabilism faces two well-known challenges. One springs from Pollock (1984) and the other from Feldman (1985). Neither amounts to the Content Complaint. And nor does their fusion. Consider each in turn.

Belief-forming processes are reliable in some-but-not-all contexts. Process Reliabilism must tell us which matter. It must motivate and specify the contexts in which reliability is to count. Call this the *Reliability-Where* problem.

Similarly, belief-forming processes can be accurately described in countless ways. Your belief this book exists springs from a visual belief-forming process, a human belief-forming process, a language-related belief-forming process, an English-language-related belief-forming process, and so on. Countless descriptions work. But reliability varies across them. Process Reliabilism must tell us which descriptions matter. It must motivate and specify the terms in which reliability is to count. Call this the *Reliability-of-What* problem.

Both problems can be solved by Teleology. And their solution turns on a pair of interlinked claims:

(A)   Certain physical structures were designed by Nature to generate beliefs;

and

(B)   They were designed to do so in certain contexts.

Neither (A) nor (B) is conceptually true. But they're true all the same. We know enough about our place in Nature to be confident, for instance, that visual-belief-forming processes were designed to work in daylight on Earth. Nature grew them for that purpose.

(A) speaks to Feldman's worry and (B) to Pollock's. Nature handles both the Reliability-of-What and the Reliability-Where Problems. Process Reliabilism should say, roughly speaking, that belief is warranted when produced by mechanisms grown in virtue of their target reliability (i.e. reliability in their target context). Call such a view – augmented to echo (*) of course – Telic Process Reliabilism. It uses Nature to say not only what has to be reliable but where it must do so. This is the most natural version of Process Reliabilism.

It says nothing to counter the Content Complaint. Telic Process Reliabilism – like all Process Reliabilism – turns on nomic probability. Its reliability prescinds from local content. For this reason, the view is grossly at odds with common sense.

4.2 Recall the chance-based schema used in our discussion of Content Reliabilism:

(Φ)   E is warrant-conferring evidence for B iff **prob**(B/E) is Φ.

How should Φ be cashed? Content Reliabilism must answer this question. But it won't be easy.

For instance, assume E and B are logically independent empirical propositions. Now ask: what's the Φ such that E is warrant-conferring evidence for B iff **prob**(B/E) is Φ? An obvious proposal is

(Φ_1)   **prob**(B/E) is Φ iff **prob**(B/E) is sufficiently high.

But this can't be right. For (Φ_1) fails to ensure E probabilifies B. If sufficient height falls short of unity – which surely it must – then E may *decrease* **prob**(B) when **prob**(B/E) is sufficiently high. That should preclude (Φ_1) on Reliabilist grounds alone. An adequate analysis of warrant-conferring evidence must ensure E is such evidence for B only if E is positively relevant to B. Call this the *Relevance Constraint*.

It motivates the following thought:

(Φ_2)   **prob**(B/E) is Φ iff **prob**(B/E) > **prob**(B).

But this won't do either. The greater-than relation is too weak for our purposes. **prob**(B/E) can exceed **prob**(B) despite the former being extremely low. (Φ_2) thus fails to ensure E is strong enough evidence to play the Φ-role in (6). Specifically, (Φ_2) fails to ensure E produces *prima facie* warrant which ripens into *ultima facie* warrant when unperturbed by background evidence. An adequate analysis of warrant-conferring evidence must secure this feature. Call this the *Strength Constraint*.

Further, (Φ_2) yields a symmetric evidential relation. E is (Φ_2)-evidence for B iff B is (Φ_2)-evidence for E. Yet that seems clearly wrong. Let

E   =   the proposition that ninety per cent of those born on Tuesday in 1950 were born by noon and Jack was born on a Tuesday in 1950;

and

B   =   the proposition that Jack was born by noon.

Suppose you learn E and nothing else intuitively relevant to B. Your credence in B should be high. E is warrant-conferring evidence for B. The reverse, however, seems wrong. Were you to learn B and nothing else intuitively relevant to E, your credence in B should not rise to the level of warrant. The flow of warrant is palpably asymmetric here. An adequate analysis of warrant-conferring evidence must allow for this possibility. Call this the *Asymmetry Constraint*.

Suppose we try a ratio. For suitable n we say

(Φ_3) **prob**(B/E) is Φ iff [**prob**(B)/**prob**(B/E) $\leq$ n].

This yields no progress. (Φ_3), like (Φ_2), passes the Relevance Constraint but fails the Strength and Asymmetry Constraints: E is (Φ_3)-evidence for B only if E probabilifies B; E may be (Φ_3)-evidence for B despite **prob**(B/E) being terribly low; and E is (Φ_3)-evidence for B iff B is (Φ_3)-evidence for E.

Suppose then we try a *difference* rather than a ratio. For suitable n we say

(Φ_4) **prob**(B/E) is Φ iff [(**prob**(B/E) – **prob**(B)) $\geq$ n].

This is progress. For with n chosen wisely, all three Constraints are satisfied:

(a)   E is (Φ_4)-evidence for B only if **prob**(B/E) > **prob**(B).
(b)   E is (Φ_4)-evidence for B only if **prob**(B/E) is sufficiently high.
(c)   Only when **prob**(E) = **prob**(B) is (Φ_4)-evidence symmetric.

But notice: the Strength Constraint is satisfied by requiring **prob**(B) to be low. The difference between **prob**(B/E) and **prob**(B) is greater than or equal to n only if **prob**(B) is *less than* or equal to (1–n). **prob**(B/E) is sufficiently high only if **prob**(B) is sufficiently low. That's odd. What is not clear is how to avoid such oddities in a Φ-based analysis of warrant.

4.3 The use of truth in the norm-box story requires two comments. First, it is purely deflationary. One desires truth in the relevant sense just if there's a question about proposition $\varnothing$ and one desires to believe $\varnothing$ iff $\varnothing$. Examples: one might desire to believe snow is white iff snow is white; one might desire to believe AC Milan are terrific iff AC Milan are terrific. For short: one might desire to believe the truth. This is a patently deflationary usage of truth. See David (1994), Horwich (1990, 1998), Leeds (1978) and Quine (1970).

Second, the desire to believe truth may be a response to other desires. The norm-box story does not presuppose good reckoning springs from desire for truth-in-itself. (Nor does it rule out that thought.) The view is consistent with the idea that our deflationary desire for truth is itself a product of desire for water, food, friendship and suchlike.

4.4 Procedural norms go hand in hand with deontological normativity. This might be thought to show Reliabilism is no good. After all, such normativity underwrites the idea that 'ought-implies-can'. Many feel Reliabilism must reject that idea. Pollock and Cruz put it this way: 'What could the point of [(7)] be? It cannot be taken as a recommendation about how to reason, because it is not a recommendation anyone could follow' (1999: 140).

It's hard to see what they have in mind. For if the world is kind we can in fact undertake to be governed by norms just if they're appropriately truth related. If the world is unkind we can't do that. Pollock and Cruz seem to think the procedural face of warrant ensures 'untrumpable' capacity to fulfil its demands. They seem to think it ensures we can fulfil those demands simply by trying from within. I see no reason to buy that.

4.5 Our discussion of the Contingent Complaint echoes a good deal in Field (1996). I claim our norms are conceptually necessary. And I ground that claim in their procedural necessity. Our norms govern all reckoning contexts. Similarly, Field notes we use logic whenever we think. He points out we use logic to probe logic itself. In particular, we do so when wondering what would be the case were the logical facts different. This leads him to a startling conclusion:

(✪)   There is no cause for scepticism or puzzlement about our knowledge of logic; rather, the precondition for [sceptical doubt] is not met. (1996:371)

Why's that? Field says

(F)   we can simply make no sense whatever of the question of what we would believe were the logical facts different. (ibid.)

Since we can make no sense of the question in question, there's *no issue* about whether our logical commitments are grounded in their truth. Or so Field argues.

I think (F) is both plausible and secures (✪). But I don't think it does both at once. For (F) has a plausible and implausible reading. And only the latter secures (✪). Field leans on both readings at once. We should pull them apart. They centre on this Nozickian question:

(N)   If the logical facts were different, would our logical commitments be too?

The plausible reading of (F) says this: we cannot coherently *undertake* to answer (N). It says we cannot so much as begin. We cannot coherently get started. And this seems right. For to do so we must use logic. Answering (N) demands we govern our thought by norms we suppose are no good. This is procedurally incoherent. (N) is a question we begin to answer only by falling into such incoherence.

The implausible reading of (F) goes further. It says (N) simply makes no sense. It says (N) is *incoherent*. And if that's right, of course, it doesn't mark a cogent sceptical worry. But the claim is not credible. (N) is perfectly coherent. It's built from coherent claims with a coherent procedure. It's got from

(L)   The logical facts are as they are

and

(C)   Our logical commitments are as they are

in three steps:

(i)   negate (L)
(ii)   negate (C)
(iii)   subjunctively query the result of (ii) conditional on that of (i).

The upshot is (N): if the logical facts were different, would our logical commitments be too? This is perfectly coherent. We can make sense of the question. We can understand what's being asked. Indeed, we can grasp it well enough to see we cannot so much as begin to answer without falling into procedural incoherence.

Here one thinks of McGinn's take on the Explanatory Gap. He says there is in fact an explanation of Subjectivity in purely physical terms. But he adds we cannot grasp it. We cannot grasp the answer to a question we can sensibly pose and sensibly investigate. We're 'cognitively closed' to the answer. See McGinn (1989, 1991).

I don't buy that of course, and Chapter 2 explains why. But I do think something like it holds of (N). Specifically, I think (N) is a question we can sensibly pose but *cannot* sensibly investigate. (N) marks a blindspot in our reckoning. It probes a topic 'hyper-closed' to us. Whether our inferential commitments (as a group) are alethically grounded is *a reason-transcendent topic*. It's something we cannot profitably fathom. For to do so is to use our norms under the supposition they should not be used. And that's procedurally incoherent. It seems to me, therefore, (F) has things back to front. When it comes to our norms we can see sceptical worry is beyond our non-question-begging capacities.

Does this mean we're not warranted in using our norms? Of course not. Just think of a super-sceptic about argument. Her view is that no form of argument is OK. She distrusts deduction and induction alike. Can we convince her she's wrong? Not without begging the question. Does that mean *we're* unwarranted to infer as we do? Surely not. It just bares the limit of dialogue. Yet the same point holds for (N). That we cannot query the grounding of our norms without using them does not undermine their rightful grip on us. It just bares the limit of soliloquy.

Chapter 5

Zombies and Ghosts

5.1 The basic arguments

Zombies are special twice over. They're physically like us but lack Subjectivity. There's nothing it's like to be them. Though like you in all physical respects, zombie-you isn't like you 'upstairs'. It has no phenomenal consciousness. Its lights are out on the inside. Zombies are the undead of philosophical thought experiment. They motivate an influential argument for dualism:

	(1z)	It's conceivable that zombies exist.	{Premise}
	(2z)	If it's conceivable that zombies exist, zombies can exist.	{Premise}
	(3z)	If zombies can exist, dualism is true.	{Premise}
∴	(4z)	Zombies can exist.	{from (1z)&(2z)}
∴	(5)	Dualism is true.	{from (3z)&(4z)}

Let $\ulcorner \oplus \Phi \urcorner$ mean Φ is conceivable, $\ulcorner \Diamond \Phi \urcorner$ mean Φ is possible, Z be the zombie hypothesis, and D stand for dualism. The argument is then

[Z]

	(1z)	$\oplus Z$	{Premise}
	(2z)	$\oplus Z \Rightarrow \Diamond Z$	{Premise}
	(3z)	$\Diamond Z \Rightarrow D$	{Premise}
∴	(4z)	$\Diamond Z$	{from (1z)&(2z)}
∴	(5)	D	{from (3z)&(4z)}

[Z] is formally valid. But conceivability and possibility must each be clarified before soundness can be judged. The key is whether a sensible take can be found to make (1z)–(3z) jointly true.

Ghosts are special twice over. They're phenomenally like us but lack bodies. Though like you in all phenomenal respects, ghost-you isn't like you 'downstairs'. It has no body. Its lights are on with no inside. Ghosts are the disembodied of philosophical thought experiment. They motivate an influential argument for dualism:

	(1g)	It's conceivable that ghosts exist.	{Premise)
	(2g)	If it's conceivable that ghosts exist, ghosts can exist.	{Premise}
	(3g)	If ghosts can exist, dualism is true.	{Premise}
∴	(4g)	Ghosts can exist.	{from (1g)&(2g)}
∴	(5)	Dualism is true.	{from (3g)&(4g)}

Let G be the ghost hypothesis. The argument is then

$$[G]$$

	(1g)	$\oplus G$	{Premise}
	(2g)	$\oplus G \Rightarrow \Diamond G$	{Premise}
	(3g)	$\Diamond G \Rightarrow D$	{Premise}
∴	(4g)	$\Diamond G$	{from (1g)&(2g)}
∴	(5)	D	{from (3g)&(4g)}

[G] is formally valid. But once more conceivability and possibility must be clarified before soundness can be judged. The key is whether a sensible take can be found to make (1g)–(3g) jointly true.

We investigate in reverse order. §5.2 covers possibility. §5.3 covers conceivability. §§5.4–5 deal with arguments which employ them.

5.2 Genuine possibility

Suppose Φ can be true. This is a genuine possibility if it's a mind- and language-independent fact. Φ is genuinely possible if its possibility does not spring from how we think or talk (even in the rational ideal). Genuine possibility is like genuine actuality. It does not depend on us for its existence. It does not depend on us for its nature. Genuine possibility is a realistic domain of fact.

Ordinary practice harbours many senses of 'can'. Not all mark genuine possibility. Our practice is modally muddled. It all but obliges equivocation. We must respect it but avoid its pitfalls. Above all, we must not mistake *ersatz* possibility for the genuine item. In what follows we should highlight the type of 'can' being dealt with. We should parade that type on the surface of discussion.

To that end, consider four claims:

(1)	Water is made of oxygen and not made of oxygen.
(2)	Lincoln survived his assassination.
(3)	Gold is uncomposed.
(4)	David Lewis jumps Mount Everest in a single bound.

It's standard to assess their possibility via four criteria:

(F) The *Formal* criterion marks possibility by logical form. It says a claim can be true when it's *not* of the form ⌜Φ&¬Φ⌝. Explicit contradictions fail the test. Everything else passes. From the above list, then, (1) fails while (2) thru (4) pass. The latter three are tagged possible on the basis of their logical form. (1) is not. Let's symbolize this by underlining diamonds so generated. We have: ¬◇̲(1), ◇̲(2), ◇̲(3), and ◇̲(4). In the vernacular: (1) is not formally possible; (2)–(4) are formally possible.

(C) The *Conceptual* criterion marks possibility by conceptual content. It says a claim can be true when its falsity is not ensured by the concepts from which it's built. In other words, it says a claim can be true when full grasp of its content reveals nothing to preclude truth. Explicit contradictions fail the test. So do conceptual absurdities. Everything else passes. From the above list, then, (3) and (4) make the grade. They're tagged possible on the basis of content. A full grasp of that content reveals nothing to preclude truth. This distinguishes them from (1) and (2). A full grasp of these latter claims reveals formal/conceptual barriers to truth. Let's symbolize this by bold-facing diamonds so generated. We have: ¬◆(1), ¬◆(2), ◆(3) and ◆(4). In the vernacular: (1) and (2) are not conceptually possible; (3) and (4) are conceptually possible.

(M) The *Metaphysical* criterion marks possibility by essence. It says a claim can be true when its falsity is not ensured by the essence of its truthmakers. It says a claim can be true when the entities and features of which it speaks do not, by their nature, make the claim false. Explicit contradictions fail the test. So do conceptual absurdities. And since gold is essentially composed – let's say – (3) fails as well. From the above list, then, only (4) makes the grade. It alone gets tagged possible on the basis of the metaphysics of its subject matter. Let's symbolize this by starring diamonds so generated. We have: ¬◇*(1), ¬◇*(2), ¬◇*(3) and ◇*(4). In the vernacular: (1)–(3) are not metaphysically possible; (4) is metaphysically possible.

(N) The *Nomic* criterion marks possibility by natural law. It says a claim can be true when its truth is not prevented by such law. Explicit contra-dictions, conceptual absurdities, and metaphysical slip-ups fail the test. Claims like (4) do as well. Natural law precludes Lewis jumping Mount Everest. Let's symbolize this by dotting diamonds so generated. We have: ¬◇̇ (1), ¬◇̇ (2), ¬◇̇ (3) and ¬◇̇ (4). In the vernacular: (1)–(4) are nomically impossible.

The formal mark of possibility applies to (2)–(4). The conceptual mark applies to (3) and (4). The metaphysical mark applies to (4) alone. And the nomic mark applies to none of the claims.

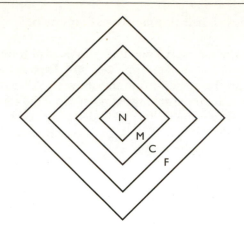

Figure 5.1

This illustrates something important. The pat criteria used to mark possibility *nest*. Satisfaction of (N) implies that of (M). Satisfaction of (M) implies that of (C). Satisfaction of (C) implies that of (F). But not the other way round. We may picture the received view as in Figure 5.1.

Here's a heuristic. Start with claims in a bag. Think of modal criteria as filters. Dump the bag through the filters. The formal one lets most everything through. It's extremely coarse-grained. Conceptual, metaphysical and nomic filters winnow out more and more claims. Diamonds nest as in Figure 5.1. Our job is to see which criteria mark genuine possibility.

I work with the standard view. It says

> (i)   The Formal criterion does *not* mark genuine possibility;
> (ii) The Conceptual criterion does *not* mark genuine possibility;
> (iii) The Metaphysical criterion *does* mark genuine possibility;
> and (iv) The Nomic criterion *also* marks genuine possibility.

Let's take each in turn.

(i) The Formal criterion

Suppose Ψ's logical form is $\ulcorner\Phi\&\neg\Phi\urcorner$. The claim fails (F). In the event, there'll be no genuine possibility Ψ is true. Its logical form precludes truth. But suppose Ψ passes (F) rather than fails. Does that ensure genuine possibility for it?

No. Recall

> (2)   Lincoln survived his assassination.

This claim satisfies (F). Its logical form is not $\ulcorner\Phi\&\neg\Phi\urcorner$. Yet no genuine possibility involves surviving assassination. It's genuinely impossible to do that. Let $\ulcorner\blacklozenge\Phi\urcorner$ stand for Φ's genuine possibility. We have

$$\lozenge(2) \ \& \ \neg\blacklozenge(2).$$

(2) is formally possible but genuinely impossible. The Formal criterion does not mark genuine possibility. $\lozenge$ does not entail $\blacklozenge$.

(ii) The Conceptual criterion

Suppose full grasp of Ψ reveals something which precludes truth. The claim fails (C). In the event, there'll be no genuine possibility Ψ is true. Example: full grasp of (2) reveals conceptual conflict which precludes truth. There's no genuine possibility Lincoln survived assassination. Yet what goes for (2) goes for all (C)-failing claims. If Ψ's 'conceptual form' precludes truth, there's no genuine possibility Ψ is true. On the other hand, suppose Ψ passes (C) rather than fails. Does that ensure genuine possibility for it?

No. Consider

(6)   David Lewis is Bruce LeCatt.

David Lewis is a famous philosopher. So-called he authors many books and articles. Bruce LeCatt is the so-named author of one little paper. Nevertheless, David Lewis is Bruce LeCatt. Lewis and LeCatt are one person.

There's no genuine possibility (6) is false. So there's no genuine possibility its negation is true. There's no such possibility that

$\neg$(6)   David Lewis is not Bruce LeCatt.

Yet $\neg$(6) passes (C). Its full grasp reveals nothing to preclude truth. Indeed, I should imagine many accept $\neg$(6). Their credulity is fixed, however, to a claim with no genuine possibility of truth. That $\neg$(6) is false – much less perforce so – transcends its own full grasp. Such grasp reveals neither the claim's truth value nor its modal status. $\neg$(6) is conceptually possible yet genuinely impossible.

Or consider the old chestnut

(7)   Water is H_2O.

There's no genuine possibility (7) is false. Hence there's no genuine possibility its negation is true. Yet this fact is not revealed by full grasp of $\neg$(7). Nothing in such grasp precludes truth. $\neg$(7) is conceptually possible yet not genuinely possible. The conceptual criterion does not mark genuine possibility. $\lozenge$ does not entail $\blacklozenge$.

Objection

> (C) is unworkably imprecise. What is it, after all, for the
> falsity of a claim to be ensured by concepts from which it's
> built? What is it for grasp of concepts to reveal something
> which precludes truth?

> Fair enough. We need a theory of conceptual grasp. We
> need one here, and we'll need one later. It's disappointing
> to realize, then, that the theory of concepts is massively
> underdeveloped. The philosophical literature is in post-
> Twin-Earth disarray. And the scientific literature is in its
> infancy. At this stage we must work with what we've got:
> intuition. Yet that tool suggests conceptual possibility does
> not mark genuine possibility.

(iii) The Metaphysical criterion

Suppose the objects and features which form Ψ's subject matter have
natures which preclude truth. This means Ψ fails (M). In the event, there'll
be no genuine possibility Ψ is true. But suppose Ψ passes (M) rather than
fails. Does that ensure genuine possibility for it?
    Yes. Consider

(8)   Something moves at superluminal velocity.

This claim satisfies (M). It's falsity is not ensured by the essence of its truth-
makers. The entities and features of which it speaks do not, by their nature,
render (8) false. Admittedly, superluminal velocity contravenes natural law
(as we understand it). But nothing in the nature of being or movement
makes that so. Their essence permits superluminal velocity. We have

$$\Diamond{*}(8) \ \& \ \blacklozenge(8)$$

(8) is metaphysically and genuinely possible. But what goes for (8) goes for
all (M)-passing claims. The Metaphysical criterion marks genuine possibility. $\Diamond{*}$ entails $\blacklozenge$.

Objection

> Properties are individuated by their place in natural law.
> Such law precludes superluminal motion. The property of
> movement, therefore, *is* individuated so that such motion is
> precluded. Superluminal velocity is metaphysically impos-

sible. You haven't shown metaphysical possibility can go with nomic impossibility.

At most this shows (M) and (N) come to the same thing. It does not show they fail to mark ◆. Even if there's no genuine possibility of passing (M) but failing (N), that impugns neither as a mark of ◆. It just translates the presently-relevant issue about (M) into one about (N). It means (M) marks ◆ exactly if (N) does.

(iv) The Nomic criterion

Natural law precludes superluminal movement. (8) fails (N). On certain views of property individuation, then, there's no genuine possibility (8) is true. But let's not commit to those here. Let's leave it open whether failing (N) precludes ◆. The crucial issue for us is whether passing (N) marks ◆. So suppose Ψ passes (N). Does this ensure genuine possibility for it?

Yes. Consider

(9)   There are nine people over nine feet tall.

This claim satisfies (N). The existence of such people does not contravene natural law. Though doubtless false, the truth of (9) would not be miraculous. It would just be unusual. We have

$$\Diamond(9) \ \& \ \blacklozenge(9)$$

(9) is nomically and genuinely possible. But what goes for (9) goes for all (N)-passing claims. The Nomic criterion marks genuine possibility. $\Diamond$ entails ◆.

(F) and (C) fail where (M) and (N) succeed. The former do not mark genuine possibility. The latter do. In the vernacular: formal and conceptual possibility are not genuine possibility; only metaphysical and nomic possibility are the genuine item.

5.3 Conceivability

Perhaps the murkiest notion at work in [Z] and [G] is conceivability. One reason for this is simple. It tags a disparate range of mental activity. We should distinguish states within the range. Then we should see whether conceivability can perform its allotted work in the arguments.

By and large, conceivability springs from *experiential imagination*. There are four ways it may do so. The structure they share is this:

(*)   Φ is conceivable for S because   (a) S puts herself in a state of sensuous imagination;
(b) it has feature F; and
(c) F stands in relation R to Φ.

Four examples:

(I) Let Φ be the claim that S raises her right hand palm inward. Suppose Φ is conceivable for S. This might consist in S visually imagining her right hand being raised palm inward. In the event, (*) is applicable. Its sensuous imagination is visual imagination. F is having Φ as content. And R is identity. Φ is conceivable for S through an act of *direct imagination*. Φ is conceivable for S because she visually imagines Φ.

(II) Let Ψ be the claim that H_2O floats in blue sky. Let θ be the claim that a cloud floats in blue sky. Suppose the former is conceivable for S. This might consist in visually imagining the latter. (*) covers this case less directly than before. Its sensuous state is once more visual imagination. F is now having θ as content. But R is not identity. Rather, it's a theory-mediated confirmation relation. Ψ is conceivable for S not by directly imagining Ψ but by directly imagining something which confirms Ψ by S's lights. Ψ is conceivable for S through an act of *evidential imagination*. Ψ is conceivable for S because she directly imagines something which confirms Ψ by her lights (namely θ).

(III) Let Γ be the claim that S has pain in her right hand. Suppose Γ is conceivable for S. This might consist in S imagining herself with such pain. In the event, S's imaginative state will be like the one it renders conceivable. Her imaginative state will *phenomenally resemble* pain in her right hand. And the more vivid her imagination the more it will do so. Here (*) applies rather differently than before. Its sensuous state is one of proprioceptual imagination. F is a phenomenal feature (or range of such features). And R is a relation of resemblance. Γ is conceivable for S through an act of *phenomenal simulation*. Γ is conceivable for S because she puts herself in a state of sensuous imagination which phenomenally resembles Γ's truthmaker.

(IV) Let 𝒫 be the hypothesis that S's painful right hand is raised palm inward. Suppose 𝒫 is conceivable for S. This might consist in the joint realization of imaginative states as in (I) and (III). After all, 𝒫 is the combination of Φ and Γ. S might visually imagine her right hand being raised palm inward, proprioceptively imagine pain in that hand, and thereby find 𝒫 conceivable. (*) applies combinatorily. Its sensuous imagination is a combination of visual and proprioceptive imagination. F is a combination of having Φ as content and having phenomenal properties. And R is a combination of being one part of 𝒫's logical form and phenomenally resembling the other part's truthmaker. 𝒫 is conceivable for S through joint acts of direct imagination and phenomenal simulation. 𝒫 is conceivable for S because she directly imagines Φ while phenomenally simulating Γ. Conceivability springs from *imaginative splicing* (or 'splicing' for short).

Now, it's natural to think zombies and ghosts are conceivable because we enjoy experiential imagination. But this isn't so. Only ghosts are conceivable for this reason. Such imagination does not explain the conceivability of zombies. They are in fact conceivable. But that is not because they're experientially imaginable. Consider each in turn.

Ghosts combine phenomenology with lack of embodiment. We can imagine them by combining phenomenal simulation and evidential imagination. Here's Bill Hart's vivid recipe:

> Suppose that one morning, still embodied, you awaken. Before raising your eyelids, you grope your way over to your mirror. Facing it, you raise your lids; you can see in the mirror that your eye sockets are empty, that your eyeballs are missing; the point is that you can visualize your face with empty eye sockets as it would look to you in the mirror. This is, of course, curious. So raising your hand, you probe an empty eye socket with one of your little fingers. You can visualize how that little finger probing the socket would look . . . Growing more curious, you saw round the top of your head, peel back the top of your skull, and peer into your brain pan; it, too, is empty, and again the point is that you can visualize how your empty brain pan would look to you in the mirror . . . Moreover, you can visualize what you would see in the mirror even if all the rest of your body were gone . . . So you have a recipe for visual experience of yourself disembodied. (1988, 52–3)

In this scenario you directly imagine having a visual impression. That impression depicts the world a certain way. By your lights, such a depiction is evidence of disembodiment. Were you to have a body, after all, you'd see it in the mirror. Further, your direct imagination phenomenally simulates the visual impression of which it's an imagination. What it's like visually to imagine things looking thus and so phenomenally resembles what it's like for them to look thus and so. A single act of visual imagination does two things at once. It phenomenally simulates a visual impression. It evidentially simulates disembodiment. It thereby renders ghosts conceivable.

Now embellish the story. Suppose you wake with a stinking hangover. You have bedspins, queasiness, fever. Then Hart's scenario runs as before. This too renders ghosts conceivable. It splices together

(a) direct visualization of how things would look were you to gaze in a mirror while invisible;

and

(b) phenomenal simulation of that visual experience together with symptoms of hangover.

This bit of imaginative splicing renders *hungover* ghosts conceivable. I take it as given, then, that ⊕G can grow from experiential imagination. One reason why ghosts are conceivable is because we can evidentially imagine them.

Nothing like that works for zombies. They combine physical natures with a lack of phenomenology. For short: they combine body and no mind. Experiential imagination cannot coherently capture this combination. To see why, let ⌜(B&¬M)⌝ label it. Four points are then relevant. They match (I)–(IV) above:

(i) Although we can imagine directly observing B – or near enough anyway – we cannot imagine so observing ¬M. Neither phenomenology nor its absence is directly observable. We cannot imagine so observing (B&¬M). We cannot directly imagine zombies. The most we can do is so imagine their bodies.

(ii) Although we can imagine directly observing B – or near enough anyway – and we can imagine directly observing something which confirms ¬M – say a rock on the ground – we cannot coherently imagine both descriptions applying at once. For directly observing B itself confirms M. To imagine so observing is to imagine something which undercuts ¬M. Remember: to count as a zombie something must combine a physical nature which we take to ground consciousness with a lack of consciousness. For this reason, we cannot evidentially imagine zombies. The most we can do is so imagine each part of their definition separately. Once those parts go together, an incoherent whole results. It's possible to imagine directly observing something which would, by someone else's lights, confirm the existence of what one considers a zombie. But it's *not* possible to imagine directly observing something which would, by one's own lights, confirm the existence of what one considers a zombie. Zombies are not evidentially imaginable.

(iii) It's an open issue in this context whether physical and phenomenal features are one. It's thus open whether we can phenomenally simulate B. If type physicalism is true, that might be possible. But it's not open whether we can phenomenally simulate ¬M. That we cannot do. ¬M is the absence of phenomenology. To simulate it would be to put oneself in an experiential imaginative state like nothing at all. And that's impossible. Experiential imagination cannot be like nothing. To be experiential is to be phenomenal. To be phenomenal is to be like something. No state can be like something and also like nothing. We cannot phenomenally simulate zombies. The most we can do is be their phenomenal counterparts.

(iv)   Although we can directly and evidentially (and perhaps even phenomenally) simulate B, and we can also evidentially imagine ¬M, we cannot coherently splice the pieces together. The former are in tension with the latter. As we have just seen, experiential imagination which grounds B undercuts experiential imagination which grounds ¬M. Splicing them yields incoherence.

Conclusion: we can neither directly imagine, evidentially imagine, phenomenally simulate nor splice together zombies. We cannot base their conceivability on experiential imagination.

This means $\oplus Z$ is 'purely conceptual'. We find the zombie hypothesis conceivable by grasping its components, reflecting on their place within Z's logical form, and discerning no incoherence. Z's conceivability springs from lack of conceptual conflict. A claim's conceivability is purely conceptual, then, if it satisfies the Conceptual criterion. But this means (C)-based conceivability is just conceptual possibility. So $\ulcorner \Diamond \Phi \urcorner$ shall henceforth tag Φ's (C)-based conceivability as well as its conceptual possibility. When Φ's conceivability springs from experiential imagination, we'll write $\ulcorner \oplus_{EI} \Phi \urcorner$.

5.4 Rejecting the arguments

We have two wells of conceivability: conceptual reflection and experiential imagination. Both ground that of ghosts. Only the former grounds that of zombies. [Z] and [G] require conceivability to secure genuine possibility. We're left with three arguments. One grows from Z's conceptual possibility:

$$[\Diamond Z]$$

(1z)	$\Diamond Z$	{Zombies are conceptually possible.}
(2z)	$\Diamond Z \Rightarrow \blacklozenge Z$	{Zombies are conceptually possible only if they're genuinely possible.}
(3z)	$\blacklozenge Z \Rightarrow D$	{Zombies are genuinely possible only if dualism is true.}

∴ (4z)   ◆Z   {Zombies are genuinely possible, from (1z)&(2z).}

∴ (5)   D   {Dualism is true, from (3z)&(4z).}

One grows from G's conceptual possibility:

$$[\Diamond G]$$

(1g) $\Diamond G$ {Ghosts are conceptually possible.}

(2g) $\Diamond G \Rightarrow \blacklozenge G$ {Ghosts are conceptually possible only if they're genuinely possible.}

(3g) $\blacklozenge G \Rightarrow D$ {Ghosts are genuinely possible only if dualism is true.}

∴ (4g) $\blacklozenge G$ {Ghosts are genuinely possible, from (1g)&(2g).}

∴ (5)   D   {Dualism is true, from (3g)&(4g).}

And one grows from G's experiential imaginability:

$$[G_{EI}]$$

(1g)* $\oplus_{EI} G$ {Ghosts are experientially imaginable.}

(2g)* $\oplus_{EI} G \Rightarrow \blacklozenge G$ {Ghosts are experientially imaginable only if they are genuinely possible.}

(3g) $\blacklozenge G \Rightarrow D$ {Ghosts are genuinely possible only if dualism is true.}

∴ (4g) $\blacklozenge G$ {Ghosts are genuinely possible, from (1g)&(2g).}

∴ (5)   D   {Dualism is true, from (3g)&(4g).}

The question is simple: are the arguments sound?

Well, we can already see [$\Diamond Z$] and [$\Diamond G$] have *at most* two correct premises. For we know conceptual possibility is not the genuine item. Φ can be conceptually possible yet genuinely impossible. Recall our example:

¬(6)   David Lewis is not Bruce LeCatt.

This claim is perfectly coherent. A full grasp of its content reveals nothing to preclude truth. ¬(6) is conceptually possible. Yet there's no genuine possibility it's true. Conceptual possibility does not secure genuine possibility. Neither the conceptual possibility of zombies, nor that of ghosts, secures their genuine possibility. (2z) and (2g) are false. [$\Diamond Z$] and [$\Diamond G$] are unsound. Though formally valid, they endorse bogus sufficient conditions for genuine possibility.

That leaves (2g)*. The question is whether experiential imaginability secures genuine possibility. Does $\oplus_{EI} G$ imply $\blacklozenge G$?

A pair of examples show the answer is *no*:

(a) Consider a sequence of drawings attached to a pinwheel. Let each depict genuine possibility. The contraption generates 'moving pictures' when spun. Let them depict a conceptually incoherent story. When spinning, the pinwheel's drawings are a diachronic representation. The temporal segment depicted is shown to be filled with conceptual incoherence. Let the story shown be S.

S is experientially imaginable. We can imagine looking at the spinning pinwheel. Hence

$$\oplus_{EI}S \ \& \ \neg\Diamond S.$$

S is experientially imaginable but conceptually impossible. The standard view has it, however, that genuine possibility implies conceptual possibility. For its weakest mark (M) does. Conceptual slip-ups are not genuinely possible. Hence

$$\blacklozenge S \Rightarrow \Diamond S.$$

But now we have

$$\neg\blacklozenge S.$$

S is experientially imaginable but not genuinely possible. $\oplus_{EI}$ does not entail $\blacklozenge$.

(b) Consider *Print Gallery* by Escher. It depicts a print gallery whose patron views a print depicting the very space inhabited by the viewing patron. That's conceptually impossible. If something inhabits the space depicted by a print, it's an intentional object. No such object can gaze upon its ur-intentional depiction. The story of *Print Gallery* is a conceptual slip-up. Let that story be E.

E is experientially imaginable. Just shut your eyes and imagine *Print Gallery*. It follows that

$$\oplus_{EI}E \ \& \ \neg\Diamond E.$$

E is experientially imaginable but conceptually impossible. So as before we have

$$\blacklozenge E \Rightarrow \Diamond E$$

and thus

$$\neg \blacklozenge E.$$

Once again experiential imaginability does not secure genuine possibility. $\oplus_{EI}$ does not entail $\blacklozenge$.

(a) and (b) show (2g)* is false. $\oplus_{EI}G$ does not entail $\blacklozenge G$. The experiential imaginability of ghosts does not secure their genuine possibility. $[G_{EI}]$ is unsound. Like $[\lozenge Z]$ and $[\lozenge G]$, it relies on a bogus sufficient condition for genuine possibility. The former utilize conceptual possibility. $[G_{EI}]$ deploys experiential imaginability.

This suggests zombies and ghosts are a red herring. More specifically, it suggests no useful argument for dualism springs from them. As we're about to see, however, that's quite wrong. One useful argument springs from the ashes.

5.5 Common-sense ghosts

Conceptual coherence and experiential imaginability are insufficient for genuine possibility. That much we've seen. But we've not seen they're irrelevant to such possibility. And nor could we. They're palpably relevant. Conceptual coherence and experiential imagination yield reason to think something genuinely possible. It's just that such reason is *defeasible*. Two epistemic principles codify the point:

$$(\mathcal{R}\lozenge) \qquad \lozenge \Phi \ni \blacklozenge \Phi$$

and

$$(\mathcal{R}\oplus_{EI}) \qquad \oplus_{EI}\Phi \ni \blacklozenge \Phi$$

To find something conceptually possible is reason to think it's genuinely possible. To find something experientially imaginable is reason to think it's genuinely possible. The reasons are defeasible. They can be overridden by other considerations. Both $\lozenge$ and $\oplus_{EI}$ are defeasible evidence for genuine possibility.

This suggests we try reason-based versions of [Z] and [G]. As before one grows from Z's conceptual possibility, one from G's conceptual possibility, and one from G's experiential imaginability. Let's begin with the first two.

$$\mathcal{R}[\lozenge Z]$$

(1z)	$\lozenge Z$	{Zombies are conceptually possible.}
(2z)$^{\mathcal{R}}$	$\lozenge Z \ni \blacklozenge Z$	{Defeasibly: if zombies are conceptually possible, they're genuinly possible too.}

	(3z)	$\blacklozenge Z \Rightarrow D$	{Zombies are genuinely possible only if dualism is true.}
∴	(4z)	$\blacklozenge Z$	{Zombies are genuinely possible, from $(1z)\&(2z)^{\mathcal{R}}$.}
∴	(5)	D	{Dualism is true, from $(3z)\&(4z)$.}

$$\mathcal{R}[\lozenge G]$$

	(1g)	$\lozenge G$	{Ghosts are conceptually possible.}
	$(2g)^{\mathcal{R}}$	$\lozenge G \ni \blacklozenge G$	{Defeasibly: if ghosts are conceptually possible, they're genuinely possible too.}
	(3g)	$\blacklozenge G \Rightarrow D$	{Ghosts are genuinely possible only if dualism is true.}
∴	(4g)	$\blacklozenge G$	{Ghosts are genuinely possible, from $(1g)\&(2g)$.}
∴	(5)	D	{Dualism is true, from $(3g)\&(4g)$.}

The conclusion here is supported by premises on offer. But the support it receives is defeasible. And it turns out that support is defeated.

To see why, recall the zombie hypothesis. It's a false claim. There are no zombies. At this stage, however, it's open whether there genuinely could be. So define

(DEF) $\mathcal{D} =_{df} \blacklozenge Z.$

$\mathcal{D}$ claims zombies are genuinely possible. Dualists accept it. Physicalists reject it. Unless someone is making a *conceptual* error – which, of course, they aren't – we have both

(a) $\lozenge \mathcal{D}$

and

(b) $\lozenge \neg \mathcal{D}.$

$\mathcal{D}$ and its negation are conceptually possible. It's coherent to suppose zombies are genuinely possible. It's coherent to suppose zombies are not genuinely possible. A full grasp of $\mathcal{D}$ reveals nothing to preclude truth. A full grasp of its negation reveals nothing to preclude truth.

But (a) and (DEF) combine to give

(c) $\lozenge \blacklozenge Z,$

while (c) and $(\mathcal{R}\lozenge)$ defeasibly yield

(d)　　　　　◆◆Z.

Yet the logic of ◆ then implies

(e)　　　　　◆Z.

By the same token, however, (b) and (DEF) combine to yield

(f)　　　　　◇¬◆Z.

So we also have

(g)　　　　　◆¬◆Z.

Yet the logic now entails

(h)　　　　　¬◆Z.

Therefore: conceptual reflection yields reason to accept and reject $\mathcal{D}$. It yields *symmetric defeat*. The weight conceptual possibility lends $\mathcal{D}$ counts against ¬$\mathcal{D}$; and vice versa. Conceptual evidence cancels. Full conceptual reflection sides neither with $\mathcal{D}$ nor with its negation. It symmetrically endorses each side. It thereby undercuts each side.

This means the second premise of $\mathcal{R}[◇Z]$ describes a defeated epistemic link. It's conceptually coherent to suppose zombies are not genuinely possible. This undercuts the conceptual coherence of zombies as a reason to think zombies genuinely possible. In symbols: ◇¬$\mathcal{D}$ undercuts ◇Z as a reason for ◆Z. ◇¬$\mathcal{D}$ undercuts the ◇Z-to-◆Z link.

The same goes for ghosts. Just let

$\mathcal{D}$*　　=　　◆G

and reason as before. Once again we have symmetric defeat. The weight conceptual possibility lends $\mathcal{D}$* counts against its negation; and *vice versa*. Conceptual evidence balances. It symmetrically endorses – and thereby undercuts – each side.

This means the second premise of $\mathcal{R}[◇G]$ describes a defeated epistemic link. It's conceptually coherent to suppose ghosts are not genuinely possible. This undercuts the conceptual coherence of ghosts as a reason to think ghosts genuinely possible. In symbols: ◇¬$\mathcal{D}$* undercuts ◇G as a reason for ◆G. ◇¬$\mathcal{D}$* undercuts the ◇G-to-◆G link.

We're left with one reason-based argument for dualism. It grows from G's experiential imaginability:

$$\mathcal{R}[G_{EI}]$$

(1g)*	$\oplus_{EI}G$	{Ghosts are experientially imaginable.}
(2g)*$^{\mathcal{R}}$	$\oplus_{EI}G \ni \blacklozenge G$	{Defeasibly: if ghosts are experientially imaginable, they're genuinely possible.}
(3g)	$\blacklozenge G \Rightarrow D$	{Ghosts are genuinely possible only if dualism is true.}
∴ (4g)	$\blacklozenge G$	{Ghosts are genuinely possible, from (1g)*&(2g)*$^{\mathcal{R}}$.}
∴ (5)	D	{Dualism is true, from (3g)&(4g).}

This time defeat is not just off stage. Two remarks about why.

1. There's no chance $\mathcal{R}[G_{EI}]$ will go the way of $\mathcal{R}[\Diamond Z]$ or $\mathcal{R}[\Diamond G]$. That would involve experiential imagination yielding non-question-begging defeaters for (2g)*$^{\mathcal{R}}$. In turn that would require the genuine impossibility of ghosts to be either directly imaginable, phenomenally simulable, or spliceable together therefrom. (Theories needed to mediate evidential imagination beg the question.) But that can't happen. We can neither directly imagine, phenomenally simulate, nor splice together $\neg\mathcal{D}^*$. The genuine impossibility of ghosts is not experientially imaginable in any direct way. Such imagination does not undercut $\mathcal{R}[G_{EI}]$.

2. There's no chance (2g)*$^{\mathcal{R}}$ rests on a false general principle. For its ground is $(\mathcal{R}\oplus_{EI})$. And there's no chance $(\mathcal{R}\oplus_{EI})$ is false. It's a fact of life that experiential imagination is defeasible evidence for genuine possibility. Our modal practice is based on this fact. To question it is to undercut that practice. Remove $(\mathcal{R}\oplus_{EI})$ and no recognizable practice remains. It's a good question why experiential imagination is defeasible evidence for genuine possibility. It's *not* a good question whether it is. There's no question but that such imagination is such evidence.

We can experientially imagine ghosts. We do so from the third-person perspective via pure evidential imagination. That's what happens at cinema. We do so from the first-person perspective via evidential imagination spliced with phenomenal simulation. That's what happens in Hart-like scenarios. $(\mathcal{R}\oplus_{EI})$ thus ensures we have reason to think ghosts are genuinely possible. And we've just seen our reason is undermined by neither conceptual nor imaginative considerations. If the genuine possibility of ghosts is sufficient for dualism, therefore, we have undefeated reason to think dualism is true.

A physicalist might respond in two ways. She might locate empirical reason to endorse physicalism. This would undercut the apriori reason we've found to reject her view. Or she might deny the genuine possibility of ghosts is sufficient for dualism. This would remove a premise in our apriori reckoning. As we'll see in the next chapter, reflection on the first option reveals grounds for the second.

Discussion Points

5.1 This chapter traffics in three main areas: conceivability, concepts and modality. None are well understood. I expect debate in these areas to flourish in the immediate future, and results therefrom to augment our take on Zombies and Ghosts. This is exciting when one thinks where debate will take place. The theory of concepts, after all, is part of psychology; that of modality is part of logic/metaphysics. Meshing the areas should prove most interesting.

Here I shoot for non-trivial progress with conceivability. And I commit to realism about genuine possibility. Other than that I do one of two things: remain neutral or work with received opinion. For instance, I go with the assumption that modalities nest as in Figure 5.1. On this common-but-normally-inarticulate view: the space of formal possibility contains that of conceptual possibility; the space of conceptual possibility contains that of metaphysical possibility; the space of metaphysical possibility contains that of nomic possibility; but just the latter two are genuine; only they are mind- and language-independent modality.

I don't much like the perspective. For one thing, metaphysical modality is got through intuition bashing. One confesses intuition about essence or whatever and then form-fits metaphysical modality accordingly. By my lights, though, there's little reason to think such intuition is reliable or stable. And for this reason, metaphysical modality strikes me as a creature of darkness (to borrow a phrase from a willing lender). But nothing in this chapter hangs on that impression.

Further: Chapter 4 exposed a procedural sense of necessity which might *be* conceptual necessity. If they turn out to be one, however, the space of conceptual possibility will probably fail to contain that of genuine possibility (metaphysical or nomic). One should thus ask: is procedural modality conceptual modality?

The answer turns on how concepts are individuated. Epistemic views portend a *yes* – see Pollock and Cruz (1999) – atomistic views do the reverse – see Fodor (1998). I remain basically neutral. It seems to me we have little to work with but our pre-theoretic concept of concept. The philosophical literature is in post-Twin-Earth disarray. The psychological literature is in its infancy. Full-dress theory is yet to come. We're left with our pre-theoretic take. And it falls between a purely epistemic view and a purely atomistic one. See also Laurence and Margolis (1999), Peacocke (1995), Pessin and Goldberg (1996) and Segal (2000).

5.2 This chapter depends on the view that neither conceptual possibility nor experiential imagination secure genuine possibility. It rests on the claim, for short, that conceivability does not entail possibility.

One might defend the entailment by appeal to so-called two-dimensional semantics. On this approach, concepts have two 'readings' (or functions-to-extension – which may or may not differ). One goes with apriori matters such as conceivability. The other goes with aposteriori matters such as essence. Setting logical concepts aside, then, 'X is Y' can be heard four ways:

(i) X_1 is Y_1
(ii) X_1 is Y_2
(iii) X_2 is Y_1
(iv) X_2 is Y_2

Subscripted '1's and '2's mark when a concept is heard in the apriori/aposteriori way respectively. The machinery permits an argument:

> Conceivability and possibility do not pull apart. Appearances to the contrary deceive. Specifically, they result from projecting the modal status of readings like (ii)–(iv) onto readings like (i). If a claim is conceivable when read in the purely apriori way, however, it is possible. Or again: if a claim is conceivable when all its constituent concepts are read in the apriori way, it is possible. Conceivability secures possibility after all.

The idea here is simple: when conceivability and *im*possibility look to cohabit, that's because we 'cross read' claims. We read some constituent concepts in the apriori way and others in the aposteriori way. The result is illusion of conceivability without genuine possibility.

Now, one can motivate semantic dimensions in various ways. Three are currently popular: appeal to the theory of reference, appeal to linguistic intuition, and reflection on supposition. Each can be used to build a two-dimensional semantics. And in turn each two-dimensional semantics can be used to analyse claims like

(6)   David Lewis is Bruce LeCatt,
(7)   Water is H_2O

and their negations. Moreover, the analysis can be used to argue such claims do not break the link from conceivability to possibility. But I say the project is doomed. It's both ill-motivated and badly founded.

It's ill-motivated for this reason: we should expect conceivability *not* to secure genuine possibility. After all, such possibility is mind- and language independent. Our methods for interrogating it should turn out fallible. We should expect there to be no method of modal interrogation guaranteed to yield truth. It's one thing for thought about an objective domain to contain methods guaranteed to *preserve* truth. It's another for them to contain methods guaranteed to *yield* truth. If conceivability entails genuine possibility, however, that's exactly what conceivability is. It's a method of modal interrogation guaranteed to yield truth about mind- and language-independent fact. By my lights we should expect not to have such a method. The two-dimensional attempt to create one is ill-motivated.

And it's unfounded for this reason: no one's made clear where the dimensions come from. No one's made clear how the dimensions in question reflect competent grasp of concepts which bear them. Further, no one's explained why they should be thought capable of playing their designated role in the approach. I do not say this is impossible, of course. But I do say no one has done it. The literature is frustratingly bald hereabouts. It lacks a convincing story about why matters of aprioriticy and modality should turn on dimensions built, say, from the theory of reference.

The two-dimensional approach is pursued vigorously by David Chalmers. See work on his website, Chalmers (1996, 1998). Negative reactions to the 2D-approach can be found in Balog (2000) and Block and Stalnaker (1999), Hill and McLaughlin (1998), Loar (1998) and Yablo (1998). The foundations of two-dimensional semantics are Davies and Humberstone (1980), Evans (1979), Kaplan (1978, 1979), Lewis (1979) and Stalnaker (1978). Further discussion of conceivability, possibility, Zombies and suchlike can be found in Hill (1981, 1997, 1998), Levine (1998) and Nagel (1998), van Cleve (1983) and Yablo (1993).

Chapter 6

Physicalism and Overdetermination

6.1 The target zeitgeist

Physicalism is the view that actuality is exhausted by physical reality. Reasonable commitment to it comes in one of two ways. Either physicalism generates a world view sufficiently potent to justify its generating assumptions, or physicalism is generated by such a world view. Axiomatic physicalists occupy the first position. Argument-based physicalists occupy the second.

The former begin with physicalism. They hope a world view inspired by it will display sufficient elegance, power and scope to justify its foundations. And they might be right. Physicalism grounds the best view of certain worlds. It might do so for ours. Reasonable commitment could well spring from the axiomatic role the doctrine enjoys in a suitably potent view of actuality. At present, of course, that's not feasible. No extant theory begins to approach an effective axiomatic physicalism. Present-day knowledge makes one thing clear: reasonable commitment to physicalism requires some kind of *argument*.

A single argument combines wide currency with initial plausibility. I call it *The Overdetermination Argument*. In this chapter I subject the best version of it to scrutiny. My goal is not only to show the argument fails, but also to deflate the physicalist zeitgeist it has induced within the profession.

This mindset permeates current philosophy of mind. It forms the basis for most published work in the field, sets the framework within which students are indoctrinated, dictates the problems which must be solved, and sets the boundaries of their solution. It's grounded in a simple idea:

(*)   Physicalism flows directly from current scientific and common-sense knowledge of the world's causal structure.

I hope to expose this as myth. I aim to correct the widespread-but-mistaken impression that our causal knowledge makes physicalism the only game in town.

6.2 Locating The Overdetermination Argument

In what follows I speak of 'events' as causal *relata*. But I assume no theory of their individuation. The reason is simple. The Overdetermination Argument's power springs from its roots in our causal knowledge. The literature on causal *relata*, however, makes one thing clear: that knowledge grossly underdetermines their nature. Philosophers maintain every conceivable take on causal *relata*. They're said to be coarse-grained; fine-grained; abstract; concrete; wholly persistent; momentary; built from temporal parts; indexed to change; individuated by subjects, times, locations, properties, causes, effects, causes-and-effects. No baseline agreement exists. Every facet of causal *relata* is contentious in the extreme. Detailed views about their nature step well beyond our causal knowledge. The Overdetermination Argument *should not* turn on them. They undermine its ability to generate broadly acceptable physicalism. It's no surprise, therefore, that proponents of The Argument do not construe it as reliant upon detailed assumptions about the nature of causal *relata*. I make no such assumptions in what follows.

Now, our route to The Overdetermination Argument passes through a puzzle. The puzzle is generated by four propositions. Each recommends itself in isolation, and any three are consistent. But the four cannot jointly be true. Hence a puzzle: which three should we accept?

The structure of our puzzle permits four solutions. Each comes through accepting a troika of propositions selected from the puzzle-generating four. In turn that troika entails the negation of the odd man out. Each solution yields a three-premise *argument* against the leftover. The Overdetermination Argument is one of the solutions.

Consider, then, the appeal of four propositions:

(1) Whereas biology admits biological effects sometimes have non-biological causes, and psychology admits psychological effects sometimes have non-psychological causes – and, more generally, special science S admits S-effects sometimes have non-S causes – physics does not admit physical effects have non-physical causes. Rather, physics considers itself closed and complete. It says physical effects have their chances fully determined by physical events alone. Non-physical events play no role. Thus we have

> *Completeness of Physics*:   Every physical effect has a fully disclosive, purely physical history.

(2) Mental events have physical effects. Sometimes these are immediate – as when Gisèle's desire causes her eyebrow to quiver – and sometimes they are mediate – as when curiosity causes her to reckon further before speaking. Causal facts like these form into the common-sense view of the world. They comprise the 'manifest image'. But causal facts like these form into the

scientific view of the world too. They equally comprise the scientific image. I signal this by saying mental causes are part of the 'macro image'. Thus we have

Impact of the Mental: Mental events have physical effects.

(3) It is difficult to believe the physical effects of mental causes have distinct physical causes. Those effects would then spring from distinct sources: one mental, one physical. This seems both *ad hoc* and unmotivated. Just as the Impact claim is part of the macro image, so is the lack of such widespread overdetermination. The odd case of such overdetermination is fine. But it must be odd. (I take this for granted in what follows, often writing 'over-determination' to mean 'largescale overdetermination of physical effects of the mind'.) Thus we have

No Overdetermination: The physical effects of mental events are not generally overdetermined.

(4) Although causal interaction transpires between mental and physical events, the former do not seem a *variety* of the latter. Mental and physical events are distinct. This is how reality strikes us pre-theoretically. Thus we have

Dualism: Mental events are not physical events.

Now, each of these four propositions is compelling. And any three are consistent. Yet they cannot jointly be true. One must be dropped. Question: which should it be?

We have four arguments at our disposal:

¬(1) We might use the last three claims against the first. For if mental events have physical effects and dualism is true, but there is no overdetermination, then physical effects of mental events do not have fully disclosive, purely physical histories. This is the anti-Completeness-of-Physics argument. It concludes physics is incomplete.

¬(2) We might use the first, third and fourth claim against the second. For if physics is complete and dualism is true, but there is no overdetermination, then mental events have no physical effects. This is the anti-Impact-of-the-Mental argument. It concludes mind is physically epiphenomenal.

¬(3) We might use the first, second and fourth claim against the third. For if physics is complete and mental events have physical effects, but dualism is true, then physical effects of mental causes are overdetermined. This is the anti-No-Overdetermination argument. It concludes physical effects of the mind are largely overdetermined.

¬(4) We might use the first three claims against the last. For if physics is complete and mental events have physical effects, but there is no over-determination, then mental causes are physical causes. This is The Over-determination Argument. It concludes physicalism is true. If a currently known position generates reasonable commitment to physicalism, this is it.

6.3 Spotting a gap

Though highly influential, The Overdetermination Argument equivocates. The plausibility of the Completeness and Impact claims trade on distinct readings of 'physical'.

To see this, suppose 'physical' means *microphysical*. This equates the physical with the quantum-mechanical. The Completeness claim thus becomes:

> *Quantum Completeness*:   Every quantum effect has a fully disclosive, purely quantum history.

Physicalists claim this principle is grounded in quantum mechanics. That mechanics says quantum events have their chances fully determined by quantum states. This is said to render the scientific *bona fides* of the claim beyond question.

But notice: if 'physical' means microphysical, the Impact claim becomes:

> *Quantum Impact*:   Mental events have quantum effects.

This claim is *not* part of extant science; nor is it part of everyday experience. No working scientific theory postulates a pervasive causal link between mental events and quantum events. And neither does common sense. Quantum Impact is absent from both our theoretical and pre-theoretical image of the world. So if mental events have a pervasive causal link to quantum events, as this interpretation of 'physical' demands, an argument is needed to show they do.

On the other hand, suppose 'physical' means *broadly physical*. This equates the physical with the macro-physical plus the quantum-mechanical. On this interpretation, handshakes count as physical along with quantum events. The Impact claim thus becomes:

> *Broad Impact*:   Mental events have broadly physical effects.

As we noted in the previous section, everyday experience indicates mental events have macro-physical effects. So does macro-science. By letting 'physical' cover macro-effects, then, the causal efficacy of mind is secured by the macro image.

But notice: if 'physical' means broadly physical, the Completeness claim becomes:

Broad-Completeness: Every broadly physical effect has a fully disclosive, purely broadly physical history.

This claim is *not* part of extant science; nor is it part of everyday experience. No working scientific theory says broadly physical effects have fully disclosive broadly physical histories. And neither does common sense. Quite the contrary: both macro-science and everyday experience rely upon *mental* causes for broadly physical effects. If such effects always have broadly physical causes, as this interpretation of 'physical' demands, an argument is needed to show they do.

The dilemma, then, is this: if 'physical' means quantum-mechanical, the Completeness claim seems supported by science; but the Impact claim seems supported neither by science nor by everyday experience. If 'physical' means broadly physical, the Impact claim seems supported by science and everyday experience; but Completeness seems supported by neither. The plausibility of each trades on distinct readings of 'physical'. The Overdetermination Argument is unsatisfactory as it stands.

6.4 Closing the gap

The flaw in The Argument is simple. It tries to squeeze physicalism from competition between mental and physical causation. Yet the competition is had by theft. Since the causal efficacy of mind is secured by the macro image, while the causal hegemony of physics is secured by microphysics, we're not *guaranteed* competition between the two. After all, microphysics never mentions events found within the macro image. It never mentions handshakes, hiccups, or the felling of trees. Afortiori it never claims such events are caused by quantum states. A gap exists in The Overdetermination Argument.

To close it we need to show the causal deliverance of the macro image competes with that of microphysics. To show this we need an argument for Quantum Impact or Broad Completeness. The former would push mental causation from the macro down into the micro, thereby placing it in competition with microcausation. The latter would push microcausation up into the macro, thereby placing it in competition with mental causation.

The two levels of reality are linked, of course, by this fact:

Quantum Composition: Broadly-physical macro-events are composed of quantum events.

Handshakes, hiccups and the felling of trees are composed of quantum events. And so are other non-microphysical events. If we hope to push causation from the micro into the macro, or from the macro into the micro, we may do so by claiming causation is *closed under composition or its inverse*.

Consider the following principles. The first pushes causation downward. The second pushes it upward.

($\downarrow$)   Closure under downward composition:
            If C causes E and E is composed by E*, then
            C causes E*.

($\uparrow$)   Closure under upward composition:
            If C causes E and E composes into E*, then
            C causes E*.

($\downarrow$) says causation is preserved by the composition-of-effect relation. ($\uparrow$) says causation is preserved by the composing-of-effect relation. Each principle is sufficient, *in situ*, to patch The Overdetermination Argument.

Suppose ($\downarrow$) is true. Now consider mental event M. We may reason as follows:

> M will have broadly physical effect E, by Broad Impact; but E will be composed by quantum E*, by Quantum Composition; so M will cause E*, by ($\downarrow$); yet E* will be caused by quantum C, by Quantum Completeness; hence M and C causally compete for E*; M and C are distinct, then, on pain of large-scale overdetermination; but that's ruled out by No Overdetermination; so M and C are not distinct.

Or suppose ($\uparrow$) is true. We may reason as follows:

> M will have a broadly physical effect E, by Broad Impact; but E will be composed by quantum E*, by Quantum Composition; yet E* will have quantum-cause C, by Quantum Completeness; so C will cause E, by ($\uparrow$); hence M and C causally compete for E; M and C are distinct, then, on pain of large-scale overdetermination; but that's ruled out by No Overdetermination; so M and C are not distinct.

We have two valid arguments at our disposal:

The Downward Overdetermination Argument

Broad Impact: Mental events have broadly physical effects.
Quantum Composition: Broadly-physical macro-events are composed of quantum events.

Closure under *downward composition*:	If C causes E and E is composed by E*, then C causes E*
Quantum Completeness:	Every quantum effect has a fully disclosive, purely quantum history.
No Overdetermination:	The effects of mental events are not generally overdetermined.
∴ *QM-ism*:	Mental events are quantum events.

The Upward Overdetermination Argument

Broad Impact:	Mental events have broadly physical effects.
QM Composition:	Broadly-physical macro-events are composed of quantum events.
Closure under *upward composition*:	If C causes E and E composes into E*, then C causes E*.
Quantum Completeness:	Every quantum effect has a fully disclosive, purely quantum history.
No Overdetermination:	The effects of mental events are not generally overdetermined.
∴ *QM-ism*:	Mental events are quantum events.

These arguments close the gap spotted in the previous section. They force a causal competition between the macro and the micro. The Downward Argument does so at the micro level. The Upward Argument does so at the macro level.

Moreover, the arguments enjoin a physicalism that is both general and severe. For consider the first and last premise of each: Broad Impact and No Overdetermination. The former says mental events have broadly physical effects. The latter says these effects are not generally overdetermined. Both claims are grounded in the macro-image. Yet mental events are not *special* in this regard. That image grounds similar claims about many other events. Handshakes have broadly physical effects which are not generally overdetermined. Hiccups have broadly physical effects which are not generally overdetermined. It's plausible to suppose, in fact, that every causally significant event within the macro image has broadly physical effects which are not generally overdetermined.

This means we have argument *schemata* at our disposal. The first enjoins physicalism about ∅-events by pushing their causal efficacy down into the micro. The second enjoins physicalism about ∅-events by pushing the causal efficacy of the micro up to ∅-level. The resulting physicalism is general and severe. It covers every causally significant event from science and common sense. It reduces events within its scope to quantum mechanics.

6.5 Mereology and causal closure

Three principles before us exploit the idea that events *compose* one another: ($\downarrow$), ($\uparrow$) and Quantum Composition. As they stand the principles are blunt. The notion of composition may be sharpened in distinct ways. Each will generate a distinct Overdetermination Argument. Question: do any use plausible sharpenings of Quantum Composition and a closure principle?

Suppose we say E composes E* iff E partly constitutes E*. Here event composition is likened to proper-part-hood between substances. Just as lump of clay L might partly constitute statue S, micro-event m might partly constitute macro-event M. The idea generates partial-constitution readings of ($\downarrow$), ($\uparrow$) and Quantum Composition:

($\downarrow$-PC)   *Closure under downward partial constitution*: If C causes E and E is partly constituted by E*, then C causes E*.

($\uparrow$-PC)   *Closure under upward partial constitution*: If C causes E and E partly constitutes E*, then C causes E*.

(QM-PC)   *Quantum Partial Constitution*: Broadly-physical macro-events are partly constituted by quantum events.

This latter principle is true: broadly physical macro-events *are* partly constituted by quantum events. If ($\downarrow$-PC) is true as well, therefore, a version of the Downward Argument will beckon; and if ($\uparrow$-PC) is true, a version of the Upward Argument will beckon.

However, neither ($\uparrow$-PC) nor ($\downarrow$-PC) is true. This can be seen with thought experiments. I present three in ascending order of strength. Reflection upon them shows what an Overdetermination Argument must look like (if it's to command widespread appeal):

(E1)   1000 ducks are on a lake. All are normal save $Duck_{10}$. $Duck_{10}$ is deaf. As it happens, $Duck_{10}$ is bitten by a turtle just as a shotgun is fired nearby. The flock takes off *en masse*.

$Duck_{10}$ takes flight because of the turtle. Its flight partly constitutes that of the flock. Yet the turtle does not cause the flock to fly. The shotgun blast does. We have a counter-example to ($\uparrow$-PC). Moreover, the blast causes the flock to fly. But its flight is partly constituted by that of $Duck_{10}$. Yet the blast does not cause $Duck_{10}$ to fly. The turtle does. We also have a counter-example to ($\downarrow$-PC).

(E2)   Katie's hunger causes her to grasp an apple. At that moment, an independent chemical reaction causes a muscle in her pinkie to twitch imperceptibly.

The muscle twitches because of the chemical reaction. The twitch partly constitutes the grasp. Yet the chemical reaction does not cause the grasp. Katie's hunger does. We have a second counter-example to ($\uparrow$-PC). Similarly: Katie's hunger causes her to grasp. But her grasp is partly constituted by the twitch. Yet Katie's hunger does not cause the twitch. The chemical reaction does. We have a second counter-example to ($\downarrow$-PC).

(E3)   Mr Mogul sells his pork belly stock. This causes the market to crash. The crash is partly constituted by dealers selling their stock. This is partly constituted by Doug selling his stock, which is partly constituted by Doug making a phone call, which is partly constituted by Doug reaching for the phone, which is partly constituted by Doug lifting his arm, which is partly constituted by a muscle contraction, . . . , which is partly constituted by a chemical reaction, which is partly constituted by the decay of an atom, which is caused by an independent subatomic event.

The independent event causes the decay. The decay partly constitutes the market crash. Yet the independent event does not cause the crash. Mr Mogul does. We have a third counter-example to ($\uparrow$-PC). Similarly: the crash is caused by Mr Mogul's selling. But the crash is partly constituted by the atomic decay. Yet Mr Mogul does not cause the decay. The independent event does. We have a third counter-example to ($\downarrow$-PC).

There's a pattern here. The movement of the flock is insensitive to that of $Duck_{10}$; and *vice versa*. The grasp of Katie's hand is insensitive to the twitch in its pinkie; and *vice versa*. The state of the market is insensitive to that of the atom; and *vice versa*. In each case, events at one level are irrelevant to large- or small-scale causal patterns into which they fit. Those events needn't stand in causal relations to large- or small-scale *relata* in order for the *relata* to do so to one another. By indiscriminately chaining up or down partial constitution, then, we reach events irrelevant to the large- or small-scale patterns from which we begin. Since the events we reach are irrelevant, however, causation needn't follow us. Causation is preserved by neither downward nor upward iteration of partial constitution. In a moment we'll see why that's so.

Examples like (E1)–(E3) are constructable at will. They show when composition is likened to partial constitution, both the Downward and Upward Arguments are unsound. The former harbours the false premise that causation is closed under downward partial constitution. The latter harbours the false premise that causation is closed under upward partial constitution. If we're to press a version of the Downward or Upward Arguments, therefore, we must view composition in another way.

We may locate that way by reflecting on our *reaction* to these thought experiments. Notice (E1) seems a relatively weak counter-example to ($\downarrow$-PC) and ($\uparrow$-PC); (E2) seems relatively stronger; and (E3) seems stronger yet again. Why is that? What explains the fact that (E1) has less intuitive force than (E2), and (E2) has less intuitive force than (E3)?

The answer is this: a *conceptual link* is clearly present in (E1), is not clearly present in (E2) and is clearly absent in (E3). Specifically, it's a conceptual truth that duck-flock movements are built from duck movements; and it's 'close' to a conceptual truth that hand movements are composed of muscle movements; but it's nowhere near a conceptual truth that activity on the pork belly market is built from atomic decay.

Intuition reflects this. We're certain a blast causes a duck-flock movement iff it causes enough salient duck movements. How much is enough? Good question. But it's an empirical question. All we can say apriori is that the blast must cause enough duck movements to guarantee the flock movement. And in my view, we should be cautious about the order of explanation here. Perhaps the blast causes the flock movement by causing individual duck movements. Perhaps it's the other way around. This is not a conceptual issue. It too is an empirical issue. But the fact that duck-flock movements causally stand or fall with duck movements *is* conceptually guaranteed.

This explains why we *hesitate* over the claim that the blast of (E1) causes the flock movement in question. Since we know a salient duck movement is not caused by the blast – viz. that of $Duck_{10}$ – we pause to consider detail. We check whether the blast causes enough duck movements to count as the cause of the flock movement. When we see it does, we accept the blast as cause. Compare this with our reaction to (E2) and (E3).

We cannot be certain hunger causes a hand movement iff it causes muscle movements which constitute the hand movement. For we cannot be certain hand movements are composed of *muscle* movements. We can be certain hand movements are composed of sub-hand movements. And we know hands are composed of muscles. This is why the claim that hand movements are composed of muscle movements is overwhelmingly plausible. But such plausibility is distinct from conceptual guarantee. And this is why we hesitate less over the claim that Katie's hunger causes her grasp. Since it isn't conceptually true that muscle twitches build into grasps, the fact this twitch isn't caused by hunger gives scant reason to question hunger as cause of the grasp. This is why (E2) is a stronger counter-example than (E1).

Moreover, intuition's at sea in the pork belly case. Who knows whether Mr Mogul need cause *any* quantum decay in order to affect pork belly stock? And who knows whether causing quantum activity *in itself* is sufficient to cause pork belly activity? Intuition is silent. And so is theory. We just don't know whether economics is captured by quantum phenomena.

The essence of duck-flock movements consists in individual duck movements. This we know conceptually. Despite the former being multiply realizable by the latter, there's a recognizable sense in which duck-flock movements are nothing over and above aggregate duck movements. Here we have ontic distinctness without ontic inflation. And here we have clean conviction: causation flows back and forth across composition between duck-flock movements and duck movements. The causes of duck-flock movements cause duck movements; and the causes of duck movements cause duck-flock movements.

The essence of hand movements consists in sub-hand movements. This we know conceptually. And sub-hand movements are (*inter alia*) muscle movements. This we know empirically. Despite the former being multiply realizable by the latter, there's a recognizable sense in which hand movements are little more than muscle movements. Here we have ontic distinctness and a whiff of ontic inflation. And here we have strong conviction: causation flows back and forth across composition between hand movements and muscle movements. The causes of hand movements cause muscle movements; and the causes of muscle movements cause hand movements.

But look what we have in the pork belly case. We know the market is constituted *in some sense* by sub-atomic activity. Yet we're clueless how that's possible. We do not know whether its crash is something significant over and above that activity. The yawning conceptual gap precludes conviction. This is why we have no trouble accepting Mr Mogul as the cause of the crash despite knowing he failed to cause a quantum event which constitutes that crash. But now ask: how much difficulty would we have accepting Mr Mogul as the cause of the crash were we to learn he caused *no* quantum activity? I submit we'd have no difficulty. For the conceptual gap between microreality and the market is stupendous. It induces a perspective from which causation at each level may reasonably be thought *independent*.

The moral is this: intuition sees causation flowing across composition to just the degree it sees composition respecting an effect's essence. Intuition reflects our commitment to the Cause-and-Essence principle:

(C&E)   C causes E iff C is sufficient to bring about what's essential to E.

This is very important. Completeness of physics is found at the micro level. Efficacy of mind is found at the macro level. Overdetermination Arguments must push causation around. They must assert causation rides atop event-composition. Yet (C&E) constrains how this can be. It constrains the role composition plays within true closure principles. Specifically, it requires composition 'to stay within an effect's essence'.

This explains why both downward and upward partial constitution fail to preserve causation. Downward partial constitution permits movement from the macro to the exquisitely micro. It permits movement from an effect's essence to fine-grained events alien to that essence. For this reason, downward partial constitution fails to preserve causation. Similarly, upward partial constitution permits movement from micro to robustly macro. It permits movement from an effect's essence to coarse-grained events alien to that essence. For this reason, upward partial constitution fails to preserve causation.

6.6 The Overdetermination Argument and physics

We need an uncontentious way to locate true closure principles. As we've seen, however, the truth of such principles depends on whether the composition relation they deploy preserves an effect's essence. This means we need an uncontentious way to locate an effect's essence, and an uncontentious way to tell whether a given composition relation preserves that essence.

There's only one way to do this. Recall (E1): we know the blast causes the duck-flock movement iff it causes enough salient duck movements; and we know salience is measured by composition. Yet we don't know this on the basis of *theory*. We just see it's true. Since the conceptual distance between duck-flock movements and duck movements is nil, theory isn't required. We just see that causes of duck-flock movements cause duck movements; and we just see that causes of duck movements cause duck-flock movements. The conceptual proximity here permits knowledge at a glance. (Yet even here we find borderline cases. For example, suppose a blast causes 6 of 10 ducks to take off. Does it cause their flock to do so? The case is conceptually penumbral. For this reason, among others, the notion of conceptual distance is difficult to define. But it's something we understand. No definition is needed to know the conceptual distance in (E1) is tiny *vis-à-vis* that of (E3).)

Naturally, this is a limit case. But it's the sort of thing needed to underpin a potent Overdetermination Argument. Our confidence in a closure principle should be inversely proportional to the sum of two things: first, the conceptual distance between the domains in question; and second, the difficulty we have seeing whether the composition relation deployed stays within an effect's essence. Proponents of The Overdetermination Argument must accomplish two tasks:

(A)   Find a conceptual overlap between quantum reality and the macro-image;

and

(B)   Locate a composition relation which clearly stays within an effect's essence in the overlap.

It looks a tall order. After all, it's easy to experience vertigo when peering across the Conceptual Grand Canyon stretching from quantum reality to the macro-image. And it's easy to experience a collapse of intuition when so peering. Witness our reaction to the pork belly case. Doesn't it show (A) and (B) cannot be done?

Well, the conceptual divide between quantum reality and macroreality is great. We should be cautious in accepting unrestricted causal flow between the two. For we cannot see how quantum events build into the splendour of macroreality. We cannot see, for example, how quantum tunnelling *could* build into jalapeño peppers.

On the other hand, pork bellies and jalapeños are conceptually remote from quantum mechanics. Other aspects of the macro-image are not so far removed. For instance, both quantum reality and macroreality are shot through with spatial events. This suggests we restrict our attention to *macromovements*. Perhaps we can understand them as caused by causes of micromovements. For if the position and movement of everything micro is fixed at the micro level, while the position and movement of everything macro is fully constituted by micropositions and micromovements, then, it seems, macromovements are caused by microcauses. Within this restricted domain, therefore, the situation looks more like ducks and duck-flocks than α-particles and pork bellies.

We've reached the heart of the matter. It's no accident proponents of The Overdetermination Argument focus on movement. Their focus signals the need to satisfy (A) and (B). The best chance of doing so is with this argument:

The Upward Spatial Overdetermination Argument ('USO-Argument' for short)

(1)	*Broad Spatial Impact*:	Mental events have macrospatial effects.
(2)	*QM Full Spatial Constitution*:	Macrospatial events are fully constituted by quantum spatial events.
(3)	*QM Spatial Completeness*:	Every quantum spatial effect has a fully disclosive, purely quantum history.
(4)	*Closure under upward full spatial constitution*:	For all spatial events C, E and E*: if C causes E and E fully constitutes E*, then C causes E*.
(5)	*No Overdetermination*:	The spatial effects of mental events are not generally overdetermined.
∴	*QM-ism*:	Mental events are quantum events.

This is the best Overdetermination Argument available. What should we make of it? Does it show physicalism follows from current knowledge of the world's causal structure? Could it reasonably underpin the cocksure physicalism of our time?

No. For science itself undermines the argument. Quantum theory undermines (4), and invites speculation inconsistent with (1) and (3). As follows:

Quantum theory and (4)

The closure principle of the USO-Argument assumes macrospatial facts are conceptually similar to microspatial facts. This just isn't true. Macrospatial phenomena are radically unlike their micro counterparts. And the differences turn on two aspects of quantum theory: *superposition* and *projection*. Technical knowledge isn't needed to see how these aspects of quantum theory undermine Closure under upward full spatial constitution.

Superposition. The microspatial image is non-classical. Its 'positional space' is subject to unusual closure conditions. For example, if a particle can be located at P_1 or P_2 or P_3, then it can also be characterized by a combination such as $(1/3P_1 + 1/3P_2 + 1/3P_3)$. In the event, the particle's position is best conceived as a wave-like phenomenon described by a wave equation Ψ. This expression codifies the 'spread' of the particle over P_1–P_3. Such a particle is said to be positionally superposed.

Obviously, nothing like this occurs in the macro-image. Macropositions do not recombine so promiscuously. Just because a car could be in Houston or Dallas or Austin, say, it doesn't follow it could be sensibly characterized by $(1/3\text{Houston} + 1/3\text{Dallas} + 1/3\text{Austin})$.

Projection. Quantum theory contains two dynamical rules: the Schrödinger equation and the Projection rule. The former governs the evolution of Ψ when measurement is *not* taking place. The latter takes over during measurement. It states:

(a)　　　Upon measurement the 'spread' characterized by Ψ will *collapse* into a state such as being at P_1 or being at P_2 or being at P_3;

and

(b)　　　The system's wave function immediately after measurement will be the function Φ_n which corresponds to measured value n.

This is more than a little surprising. As one standard text puts it:

The most difficult and controversial conceptual problem in quantum mechanics concerns the nature and meaning of the quantum theory of measurement . . . The [theory states] that measurement of a physical quantity always produces a result equal to one of the [allowed values], and if the wave function is Ψ before measurement, immediately after measurement [it] will be the same as the corresponding function Φ_n . . . The effect of measurement is therefore to cause the wave function to be changed from Ψ to Φ_n. We can represent this process by

$$\Psi \longrightarrow \Phi_n.$$

measurement
giving
result n.

(Rae 1996: 238)

Obviously, nothing like this occurs in the macro-image. Macro-objects do not collapse into macrolocations upon measurement. Just because an un-observed car might be in Houston or Dallas or Austin, say, it does not follow looking will *put it* in Houston or Dallas or Austin. Quite the contrary: this is ruled out by the macro-image.

Superposition and projection are strange phenomena. The macro-image contains nothing like them. Nor *could* it and remain recognizable. For this reason, the relation between quantum reality and the macro-image is opaque. No one truly understands how the former builds into the latter. It's important to realize, however, this *isn't* merely an aspect of the Mind–Body problem. The transition from quantum reality to *macrophysical* reality is also puzzling. To pretend otherwise is to disregard the state of science. The mind-to-quantum problem is but a slice of a much larger problem: namely, that of reconciling the macro-image with quantum mechanics.

The difficulty here undermines premise (4). It shows micromovements do not stand to macromovements as duck movements stand to duck-flock movements. The cases are simply disanalogous. It's a conceptual truth that duck movements compose into duck-flock movements. But it's a puzzling fact that quantum events compose into duck movements. We know they do somehow, but we do not know how.

Premise (4) steps well beyond scientific canon. It covers superposed and collapsing events from quantum theory, and macro-events seemingly immune to these phenomena. It bridges conceptually remote domains. Since it's unclear how macromovements spring from quantum events, it's unclear causes of the latter thereby cause the former. Since quantum events do not stand to duck movements as duck movements stand to duck-flock movements, it's unclear (4) is true. The premise neither follows from science nor deserves our credence.

Measurement, (3) and (1)

The Projection rule says measurement shifts the wave function. But how? And what *is* measurement anyway?

This is the measurement problem. It lies at the heart of quantum mechanics. So-called 'interpretations' of quantum theory try to reckon, *inter alia*, what to say about quantum measurement. Often their claims conflict with the USO-Argument. Three quick examples just to make the point:

1. According to an influential reading of Bohr, collapse of the wave function is due to interaction between quantum systems and classical systems. The view goes on to claim, however, that classical systems are *irreducibly classical*. Yet if this is true, certain quantum spatial effects have non-quantum causes. For irreducibly classical systems are responsible for the collapse of the wave function. This approach to measurement is inconsistent with premise (3) of the USO-Argument.

2. According to the Subjectivism of Wigner, collapse of the wave function is due to interaction between quantum systems and consciousness. The view goes on to claim, however, that consciousness is *irreducibly mental*. Yet if this is true, certain quantum spatial effects have non-quantum causes. For irreducibly mental states are responsible for collapse of the wave function. This approach to measurement is inconsistent with premise (3) of the USO-Argument.

3. According to a 'many minds' view inspired by Everett, the wave function doesn't collapse at all. Rather, it just *appears* to collapse. What really happens in measurement is that superposition infects a brain; and when so infected, that brain generates many minds at once. The physical world, on this view, is but a giant superposed system evolving *a là* Schrödinger equation. Yet this means the physical world is not as it appears to be. For it doesn't appear to be a giant superposed system. The story is inconsistent with the macro-image. If the physical world is like *that*, minds do not have the spatial effects they seem to. This approach to measurement is inconsistent with premise (1) of the USO-Argument.

Now, there are other approaches to measurement. Some are consistent with the USO-Argument. But none has won, nor deserved to win, wide acceptance. The measurement problem is an open scientific issue. (1) and (3) turn on its solution. Their status *vis-à-vis* quantum theory is very much less than clear.

In a nutshell, then, quantum theory challenges (4) and invites speculation inconsistent with (1) and (3). Our best theory of matter undermines the USO-Argument rather than supports it.

6.7 Causal presuppositions

Despite clear counter-examples to (↑) and (↓), and real difficulties squaring restricted versions of them with physical theory, many philosophers will bury their head. 'Look,' they will say, 'we agree hand movements have macrophysical effects; and we agree those effects are composed of quantum events. It just follows that hand movements have quantum effects. Similarly,' they will continue, 'we agree quantum events have quantum effects; and we agree those effects compose hand movements. It just follows that hand movements have quantum causes. The Overdetermination Argument is fine.'

This is a mistake. From the compositional and causal facts in question it simply doesn't follow hand movements *cause* quantum events. Nor does it follow quantum events *cause* hand movements. What follows is merely that hand movements and quantum events *coincide*. It doesn't yet follow they're causally related. A view of causation is needed to forge *that* link. Non-trivial assumptions are required to get from coincidence to causation.

This is very important. To see the point clearly, consider the bromide that causation requires counterfactual activity. The familiar idea is that causal truths oblige patterns of dependence within modal reality. If this is so – and it seems hard to deny – then causal claims are doubly indexed. They're tagged to *regions* of modal reality and to *patterns* of modal dependence. Two questions immediately press:

(a)   Are regions indexed to macrocausal claims *contained within* those indexed to microcausal claims?

(b)   Are patterns indexed to macrocausal claims *identical to* those indexed to microcausal claims?

It's clear these questions should be answered by looking to our causal/ explanatory practices. It's unclear what the answers will turn out to be. The important point for our purposes is this: a negative answer to *either* will break the entailment from coincidence to causation.

For example, suppose our causal/explanatory practices yield a negative response to (a). Perhaps causal claims in microphysics oblige counterfactual activity in a set of worlds Φ, while those of psychology oblige activity in an overlapping-but-distinct set Ψ. The picture would then be as represented in Figure 6.1.

On this model the actual world is @, Φ-worlds share our microphysics, and Ψ-worlds share our psychology. Some worlds contain quantum phenomena yet lack psychological phenomena. Others contain psychological phenomena yet lack quantum phenomena. Perhaps $(\Phi\&\neg\Psi)$-worlds yield life so alien that actual psychology doesn't apply (or no life at all). Perhaps $(\Psi\&\neg\Phi)$-worlds contain English speakers built from Democratian atoms.

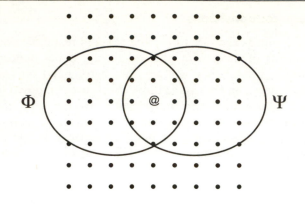

Figure 6.1

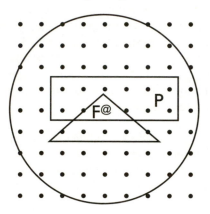

Figure 6.2

No matter which it turns out, worlds which underwrite actual causal facts *cross-classify* at different levels of scale. Causal talk between levels makes no clear sense. Causal competition simply breaks down. Despite the disunity, however, actual quantum events coincide with hand movements; and actual hand movements coincide with quantum events. What fails, at our world, is the link between coincidence and causation.

Or suppose causal/explanatory practice yields a negative answer to (b). Perhaps causal claims in micro physics oblige counterfactual pattern *F*, say, while those of psychology oblige distinct pattern *P*. Even granting a positive answer to (a), the picture would still be as represented in Figure 6.2.

Here *patterns* which underwrite actual causal facts cross-classify at different levels of scale. Causal talk between levels makes no clear sense. Causal competition once again breaks down. Despite the disunity, however, actual quantum events coincide with hand movements; and actual hand movements coincide with quantum events. What fails, at our world, is the link between coincidence and causation.

In schematic form the argument is this: suppose the claim that C causes E is indexed to pattern of counterfactual dependence P being displayed within set of worlds R. Express this with subscripts: '$[C \rightarrow E]_{P,R}$'. We may then ask of any two claims $[C \rightarrow E]_{P,R}$ and $[C^* \rightarrow E^*]_{P^*,R^*}$: is R a subset of R^*? and is P identical to P^*? If the answer to either question is *no*, the two causal claims will jointly imply neither a causal connection from C to E^* nor one from C^* to E. And this will be so no matter *how* compositional facts turn out.

Our knowledge of the world's causal structure is consistent with a *no* answer to (a). It's also consistent with such an answer to (b). Indeed, our knowledge of the world's causal structure is consistent with a *no* answer to both questions at once. The Overdetermination Argument precludes either answer along with their conjunction. It relies upon non-trivial assumptions about causation. They far outstrip current causal knowledge. For this reason, The Argument fails to show physicalism flows directly from that knowledge. It fails to show physicalism is the only respectable game in town.

This raises an interesting issue. Why is physicalism so popular? More generally, why are we prone to believe all there is to the world is the micro and its combination?

6.8 The roots of reduction

Humans live in quotidian contexts. We plan trips, cook meals, do the washing up. Our time is spent within narrow boundary conditions. Our thought needn't stray from the commonplace. Our expectation needn't stray from everyday possibility. For this reason, we're disposed to mistake the contours of quotidian possibility for those of intelligibility itself. The resulting bias, however, is a kind of modal tunnel vision. We overlook certain conceptual possibilities. We discharge others due to their alien face alone.

Now, everyday life renders common sense reductively oriented. There are four reasons why. Three are widely recognized. The fourth is not.

(A) In quotidian contexts: the large is the small writ big, and the small is the large writ small. Conceptually identical phenomena appear on different levels of scale. For instance: large-scale objects have shape, and so do their smaller cousins; large-scale objects have colour, and so do their smaller cousins; large-scale objects move, and so do their smaller cousins. Differences across level are not differences of conceptual type. They are differences of scale alone. One range of concepts is apt for both levels. Large and small are *conceptually homogeneous*.

(B) In quotidian contexts: the properties of complex objects add up from properties of their constituents. Complex synchronic facts are nothing but complexes of lesser such facts. For instance: large-scale objects have shape, but those shapes are nothing but sums of smaller-shape (and relational) facts; large-scale objects have weight, but those weights are nothing but sums of weight of smaller parts; large-scale objects have colour, but those colours are nothing but aggregations of smaller colours. In each case, bottom-up reductions exist for large-scale phenomena. Quotidian properties (and relations) are *bottom-up reductive properties (and relations)*.

(C) In quotidian contexts: macrochange is explained by microchange. Large-scale diachronic facts are produced by independent change in smaller facts. For instance: large-scale objects change shape, but those changes spring from independent change of smaller spatial facts; large-scale objects change weight, but those changes spring from independent change of smaller weights; large-scale objects change colour, but those changes spring from independent change of smaller colour. In each case, bottom-up explanation exists for large-scale change. Quotidian change is *bottom-up change*.

(D) In quotidian contexts: a property is realized by other properties *only if* it's realized whenever it could make an appearance. A property is always realized or never realized. Realization is all or nothing. For example: large shapes are realized by lesser shapes throughout everyday possibility; large weights are realized by lesser weights throughout everyday possibility; and large colours are realized by smaller colours throughout everyday possibility. In each case, a quotidian realizee never appears unrealized; and nor could it within everyday life. Such properties are realized throughout everyday possibility. They show *modally invariant realization*.

Within the sphere of quotidian possibility, then, reality is conceptually homogeneous across levels of scale, filled with bottom-up reductive properties, bottom-up explicable change, and modally-invariant realization. These are the roots of reductionism. Common sense is reductively oriented because (A)–(D) characterize everyday life. They generate reasonable expectation that large builds from small without remainder. Within quotidian life, after all, that's how things work.

6.9 Pulling the roots

(A)–(D) needn't have characterized reality. Consider how things might have been:

¬(A): It's not necessary that large and small facts are conceptually homogeneous. One way to state Sellars' puzzle, in fact, is in just these terms:

quotidian facts and microscientific facts are conceptually heterogeneous. The concepts involved in their canonical conception seem starkly unrelated. For this reason, one wonders how microscientific facts add up to quotidian facts. One wonders whether the two blend into one reality. The puzzle has bite precisely because conceptual homogeneity prompts reductionism. Once it's lost – as we find across the manifest and scientific divide – the viability of reductionism is unclear. Not only is it unnecessary that large and small are conceptually homogeneous, then, it's not even *true* they're so homogeneous.

¬(B): It's not necessary that properties are bottom-up reductive. After all, it's one thing for a property instance to be small. It's quite another for it to be basic. The former issue concerns scale alone. The latter concerns whether the instance is something over and above other facts, whether it belongs in the minimally complete description of things.

The issues pull apart. They generate four conceptual possibilities: a property might be large-scale and basic, large-scale and reductive, small-scale and basic or small-scale and reductive. The first three are relatively uncontentious. The fourth normally goes unmentioned.

But consider the colour-cube world. In it substantivalism about space is true. And colours are fundamentally instanced by one-cubic-foot regions of space. There are pink cubes and blue cubes and yellow cubes, say. And they perdure: cubes persist by having temporal parts. Further, cubes have their own mechanics. Their creation, destruction and movement is fully described by closed theory. Smaller-scale facts don't come into it. But there are such facts in this world. Small tiles move about which are normally invisible. They have no colour. When one slots into the surface space of a cube, however, its surface instantly *participates* in the colour instance of that cube.

In such a world, large- and small-scale colour facts are conceptually homogeneous. But the latter reduce to the former. Small-scale colour facts are nothing over and above large colour facts in which they participate. We have top-down reduction of colour. We have top-down reduction of conceptually homogeneous properties. Not only is it unnecessary that properties are bottom-up reductive, then, it's unnecessary that conceptually homogeneous properties are so reductive. Our quotidian world isn't like that, of course; but it might have been.

The point does not rest on the coherence of colour playing its role in this story. It rests merely on the intelligibility of that role. Even if colour cannot sensibly fill its role in the colour-cube world, it's a sensible role to fill. It's intelligible that properties fill it. No incoherence results from the thought that large-scale property instances explain their smaller-scale cousins. Perhaps such properties make no appearance in our world. Perhaps they're alien properties. That doesn't matter. What matters is that properties can sensibly fill their role in the colour-cube world. It's conceptually possible.

And when they do, we have top-down reduction of conceptually homogeneous properties. It's unnecessary that properties are bottom-up reductive.

¬(C): It's not necessary that change is bottom-up explicable. After all, it's one thing for change to be small. It's quite another for it to be basic. The former concerns scale alone. The latter concerns whether it belongs to the minimally complete list of explainers.

The issues pull apart. They generate four conceptual possibilities: a change might be large-scale and basic, large-scale and derivative, small-scale and basic, or small-scale and derivative. Here too the first three are more widely recognized than the fourth. But we can easily see how to make sense of the latter. Just augment the colour-cube story: add that cube and tile movements relate so that changes of tile colour are due to cube movements. When a tile goes from pink to blue, say, that fact springs from colour-cube movement. Small shifts of colour are produced by large shifts in colour. Small colour change is derivative. It tags along with colour-cube movement.

Or consider the box-and-ball world. In it there are large-scale boxes and small-scale balls. The boxes have their own mechanics. Their creation, destruction and movement is fully described by closed theory. Small-scale facts don't come into it. Further, balls remain still unless their centre occupies that of a box. When that happens, the centrepoints remain coincident. Balls move because boxes do.

In such a world, large- and small-scale movements are conceptually homogeneous. But the former yield the latter. We have top-down explanation of movement. We have top-down explanation of conceptually homogeneous change. Not only is it unnecessary that change is bottom-up explicable, then, it's unnecessary that conceptually homogeneous change is so explicable. Our quotidian world isn't like that, of course; but it might have been.

Once again the point rests on the intelligibility of the example's form. Even if colours cannot sensibly fill their role in the dynamic colour-cube story, and even if box and ball movements cannot sensibly fill their role in the box-and-ball story, the roles are nevertheless sensible. It's intelligible that properties fill them. No incoherence results from the idea that large-scale change explains small-scale change. Perhaps such change makes no appearance in our world. Perhaps it's alien change. That doesn't matter. What matters is that change can fill its role in these stories. It's conceptually possible. And when it does, we have top-down explanation of change. It's unnecessary that change is bottom-up explicable.

¬(D): It's not necessary that realization is modally invariant. A property might be basic in some worlds and derivative in others. So far as intelligibility goes, in fact, a property might be basic and derivative in one world. Were that to happen, some but not all of its instances would belong to the minimally complete description of things.

Take dispositions. Orthodoxy says they need categorical realizers. If correct, they show modally invariant realization. But orthodoxy doesn't seem right. For it's coherent that dispositions are realized by other dispositions. There's no conceptual need for categorical realizers. Indeed, it's even coherent that *bottom-rung* dispositions are basic, that they simply go unrealized. And if one were to appear elsewhere in a world's realization hierarchy, some but not all of its instances would be basic. Some but not all would belong to the minimally complete description of things. The disposition would be basic and derivative in one world. The idea is perfectly coherent.

For example, large-scale objects spin; and they do so derivatively. Their spin consists in cross-temporal relations between smaller-scale parts. Their spin is realized phenomena. The spin of electrons, however, isn't like that. It does not consist in cross-temporal relations between smaller-scale parts. Electrons have no smaller-scale parts; afortiori they lack parts which realize spin. Spin is basic and derivative in the actual world. Some but not all of its instances belong to the minimally complete description of things.

Some will say two notions lie behind the single word 'spin': everyday spin and scientific spin. They'll say the former is conceptually tied to realization while the latter is not. They'll insist 'spin' takes different truth-makers in science and everyday life. On their view, a single word stands for distinct phenomena within distinct explanatory practices. If that's right, 'spin' doesn't name a property which makes basic and derivative appearances in reality.

But it doesn't seem right. After all, it's no accident the everyday word gained use in microphysics. Spinning electrons and baseballs take one quantified treatment (via the so-called rotation group). And just as electron spin helps explain electron movement in a magnetic field, baseball spin helps explain curveballs, sliders, etc. The use of 'spin' in microphysics is unlike that of 'colour'. There's nothing colour-like about microphysical colour. (Roughly: microphysical colour is that upon which the strong force acts.) There's much spin-like about microphysical spin.

But even if spin cannot sensibly fill its role in the spin story, it's a sensible role to fill. It's intelligible that properties fill it. The thought that a property is basic in one world and derivative in another is coherent. So is the thought that a property is basic and derivative in one world. Perhaps such properties are alien to our world. That doesn't matter. What matters is that properties can play this role. It's conceptually possible. It's unnecessary that realization is modally invariant.

6.10 The Overdetermination Argument again

Most philosophers of mind are physicalists. But they're microreductionists too. They believe actuality is exhausted by microphysical reality. And as we've seen, they base their view on (a sanitized generalization of) [*]:

(1)   Mental events have macrospatial effects (e.g. arm movements).

(2)   Such effects are constituted by quantum spatial events (e.g. quantum tunnelling).

(3)   Every quantum spatial effect has a fully disclosive, purely quantum history.

(4)   For spatial events C, E and E*: if C causes E and E constitutes E*, then C causes E*.

(5)   The spatial effects of mental events are not generally overdetermined.

∴ (6)   Mental events are quantum events.

[*] rests on several quotidian prejudices. Some are false. Still others beg the question. And the truth value of the former undercuts the viability of the latter. To see this, consider two spots where quotidian tilt is prominent.

First, premise (4) is meant to be obvious. Yet only when large and small are conceptually homogeneous is it *obvious* that causation rides atop spatial composition. Otherwise, it's not at all obvious. In effect (4) assumes

(i)   large and small spatial properties are conceptually homogeneous,

(ii)   large spatial properties are bottom-up reductive, and

(iii)   large spatial change is bottom-up explicable.

But now we're in trouble. For consider:

•   Quotidian and quantum spatial phenomena are conceptually distinct. There's a conceptual gap between them. In fact, superposition and projection open a Conceptual Grand Canyon between the two. The large and small of [*] are conceptually heterogeneous. (i) is false.

•   (ii) assumes microreduction for large spatial facts; and (iii) does so for large spatial change. Yet [*] is meant to establish such reductionism about reality. (ii) and (iii) beg the question. They presume (some of) what [*] sets out to prove: namely, that micro-monism is true of reality.

•   Since large and small are conceptually heterogeneous, it's unclear quotidian spatial properties are bottom-up reductive, and unclear quotidian spatial change is bottom-up explicable. The truth value of [*]'s false presupposition undercuts the viability of its question-begging presuppositions. (i)'s falsity undercuts (ii) and (iii).

The details here are subtle and unsettled. But the take-home message is neither: [*] rests on unsound everyday prejudice in favour of microreduction.

Second, [*] is meant to be causally univocal throughout. (5) aims to preclude effects standing on the catching end of a single relation twice over. In turn this is meant to combine with (1)–(4) so as to entail (6). But the entailment requires quotidian and quantum causation are a *single* relation writ to different levels of scale. In effect [*] assumes

(iv)   large and small causal relations are conceptually homo-geneous,

(v)   large causal relations are bottom-up reductive, and

(vi)   large causal change is bottom-up explicable.

But now we're in trouble again. For consider:

• Causal notions make no explicit appearance in the postu-lates of quantum theory; and when they do show their face – say in application or discussion of wavepacket collapse – the notions at work are probabilistic. Orthodox quantum-theoretic causation is probabilistic causation. Quotidian causation is not. It's conceptually deterministic. That's why founding fathers of quantum theory took it to force *revi-sion* of our ordinary causal notion. Quotidian and quan-tum causation are conceptually heterogeneous. (iv) is false.

• (v) assumes microreduction for large-scale causation; and (vi) does so for large causal change. Yet [*] is meant to establish such reductionism about reality. (v) and (vi) beg the question. They presume (more of) what [*] sets out to prove: namely, that micromonism is true of reality.

• Since the large and small of [*] are conceptually hetero-geneous, it's unclear quotidian causal relations are bottom-up reductive, and unclear quotidian causal change is bottom-up explicable. Once more the truth value of a false presupposition undercuts the viability of question-begging presuppositions. (iv)'s falsity undercuts (v) and (vi).

Here too the details are subtle and unsettled. But the take-home message is neither: [*] rests on unsound everyday prejudice in favour of microreduction.

6.11 Modest physicalism

Most philosophers of mind are physicalists. But they're modally modest as well. They say reality is purely physical, but admit it might have been otherwise. When pressed to say how physicalism might have failed, how-ever, full blown reductionism shines through. The response is inevitably this:

(!)   Mental properties might have been realized by non-physical properties. They might have been realized by 'ectoplasm', for example. And if they had been, physicalism would have been false. Since mental reality isn't – but might have been – something more than physical reality, physicalism is contingently true.

Forget ectoplasm (whatever that is). But note (!)'s hardened reductionism. It allows mind to be realized by non-physical properties. But it requires mind to be realized by something. In effect (!) presupposes

(vii)   Mental properties enjoy modally invariant realization throughout all possibility.

Once (vii) is in place, (!) is the only 'modesty' left to a physicalist. Yet its reductionism about mind is decidedly immodest. Mental properties can never add to a world. They can only be realized by non-mental properties. Accord-ing to (!)-based physicalism: it's contingent that mind deflates to matter, but necessary that mind deflates. Mind is perforce an ontic free ride.

This is yet another quotidian tilt to reduction. In everyday life a property is realized somewhere only if it's realized everywhere it might show up. In general that's not so. A property can be realized in one world and basic in another. A property can be realized and basic in one world. Truly modest physicalism should make modal space for irreducibly mental facts. It should say something like

(MP)   Mental properties are realized by physical properties. But that's contingently so. They might have been realized by non-mental properties. They might have been basic. In the latter case, mental properties would have genuinely con-tributed to the world. They would have belonged to the minimally complete description of things. They don't in fact do that; but they might have.

(MP) says our world is purely physical. It also says mind could have been basic. It's a truly modest physicalism. Its absence from the literature, and the ubiquity of (!), spring from yet another unsound reductive prejudice induced by everyday life.

Discussion Points

6.1 Events and causal *relata* are hotly debated. Some of the best work can be found in Bennett (1988), Chisholm (1970), Davidson (1980, 1985), Ehring (1997), Kim (1969, 1973, 1976), Lewis (1986b), Lombard (1986), Quine (1981, 1985), van Inwagen (1978) and Vendler (1967). None agree much with one another. Indeed, the metaphysics therein is at least as contentious as physicalism itself. That's why nothing in this chapter turns on the nature of events or causal *relata*.

6.2 Four claims generate a puzzle: Completeness of Physics, Impact of the Mental, No Overdetermination, and Dualism. They're all plausible. At least one must go. The puzzle is to reckon which one. Since any three make an argument against the leftover, there are four ready-made solutions to hand.

The most popular rejects Dualism: see Hopkins (1978), Jackson (1996), Kim (1996, 1997), Loewer (1995), Papineau (1993a), Peacocke (1979), Schiffer (1987b) and Tye (1995). Some philosophers reject No Overdetermination: see Crane (1995) and Mellor (1995). Others reject Impact of the Mental: see Chalmers (1996) and Jackson (1982). (Many say Davidson is an epiphenomenalist of sorts. But it's a charge he rejects: see Davidson (1970, 1993), Honderich (1982), Kim (1993b), McLaughlin (1993) and Sosa (1993).) My view is simple: one upshot of §§6.5–10 is that Completeness is dubious when macrophysical events are at issue. Perhaps they have purely physical causes. Perhaps they don't. It's an open question.

Relevant discussion of quantum mechanics can be found in Albert (1992), Albert and Loewer (1988), Cushing (1998), Healy (1989), Hughes (1989), Rae (1996) and Wigner (1967). It makes clear one should not assume ordinary physical events are nothing over and above microphysical events. Noordof (1999) does when discussing the Overdetermination Argument. But it should not: see Sturgeon (1999). Witmer (2000) puts forth an argument for the view, and that's as it should be. But its argument rests on three dubious claims:

(i)   All macrophysical events can intervene causally at the micro level in the way macromachines do in the physics lab.

(ii)   When faced with a putative case of overdetermination, it's always better to think causes are one than to accept overdetermination.

(iii)   If macrophysical events can be nothing over and above microevents, they are nothing over and above such events. Their realization is modally invariant.

(i) neglects the very special circumstances needed to intervene scientifically at the micro level. But see Cartwright (1999).

(ii) overlooks the possibility our world contains *acceptable* amounts of overdetermination. Suppose, for instance, microphysics is complete and irreducibly macrophysical events cause one microevent each. That would guarantee many overdetermined microevents. But they would be few and far between from the micro point of view. Their macrocauses would be insignificant to a micromechanist. And were our world to be like that, in fact, it would not contain objectionable amounts of overdetermination. From both its macro and micro points of view overdetermination would be negligible. It would permit epistemic access from the macro to the micro. But it would do no more.

(iii) overlooks the possibility that realization for macrophysical events is modally variant. As §6.9 made clear, though, that's conceptually possible. Whether it's so is an open issue.

Conclusion

What we've seen

Several decades ago a great effort began to reduce Aboutness to Nature. One thing became clear over time. We have no real grip on whether the two align. We've no such grip – as I put it in the Introduction – on whether thought relates to its truth conditions like a tree to its age, a bee dance to its target, smoke to its cause, or the disjunction of suchlike. We've no real grip on correlations that may sit between Aboutness and natural fact. The reasonable position to adopt – on this issue at least – is Wait-and-See. Perhaps there's a tight fit out there. Perhaps there's not. We don't yet know. Wait-and-See.

But even if we found perfect fit between Aboutness and Nature, that would not secure physicalism. Consciousness must also be dealt with. There's an Explanatory Gap between physical and phenomenal fact. It suggests physicalism is false.

Chapter 2 showed that is not so. The Explanatory Gap has nothing to do with ontology. It's the product of phenomenal concepts. It springs from their epistemic role rather than their referent. That role prevents phenomenal concepts from figuring in pellucid property explanation. The result is an Explanatory Gap between physical and phenomenal facts so conceived which does not exist between the former and anything else.

Now, visual experience is where Aboutness and consciousness are wrapped into one. Chapter 1 plumped for the Intentional-Trope Theory. According to that view:

(a)   Veridical perceptions, illusions and hallucinations are relations of brute acquaintance between percipient and object.

(b)   The objects of brute acquaintance are private. They show their face to a single percipient.

(c)   The features of brute acquaintance are intentional features.

(d)   Instances of brute acquaintance are phenomenally typed by their feature-instance *relata*.

(e)   The features of brute acquaintance do not require, for their possession, the existence of objects or features characterized by them. They are non-object- and non-feature-involving.

The view doesn't look physicalistic. It relies on private objects, brute acquaintance and Aboutness. None are physical on their face. But they might be deep down. Appearances to the contrary mislead. Intentional-Trope Theory is compatible with physicalism. Its resources pose no principled difficulty for it.

The reason for this surfaced in Chapter 1. Theories of visual experience split into two parts: a neutral metaphysics and a phenomenal gloss. Without the latter, a view would look hopeless. The Explanatory Gap guarantees that. Without the former, a view would look vacuous. Philosophical demand guarantees that. Intentional-Trope Theory has both. Its metaphysics is spiced with phenomenal gloss. Strip it away and you have

(M)   It looks to S as if O is F just in case there's an x such that

(i)   S stands to x in an object-involving relation R;
(ii) x stands in R only to S;
(iii) R is unbuilt from mental ingredients;
(iv) x represents that O is F.

No phenomenal notions show up in (M). Indeed, only (iv) deploys mental resources. As §1.6 made clear, though, the representation therein is non-phenomenal. It characterizes conscious and non-conscious states with equal aplomb (e.g. sub-personal states posited by computational theories of vision). There's nothing essentially conscious about it. This does not automatically make it naturalistic. But it does push the notion beyond the Explanatory Gap. *This* Aboutness – unlike Scene-Immediacy – would reduce were tight-enough fit to be found between it and natural fact.

Intentional-Trope Theory is potentially physicalistic. At this stage we don't know whether it's actually so. Perhaps there are systematic correlations between its Aboutness and nature. Perhaps there are not. The reasonable position to adopt – about this issue at least – is Wait-and-See.

Consciousness poses no principled difficulty for physicalism. Neither the Explanatory Gap nor Scene-Immediacy show physicalism is false. In seeing that, though, we've not seen physicalism is true. We've just seen those who reject it on the basis of consciousness outrun their headlights. They reject a position without good cause. Reflection on consciousness leaves physicalism open. Wait-and-See.

But even if we found perfect fit between Aboutness and natural fact, and even if we saw consciousness posed no principled difficulty for physicalism, that would not secure the view. Content-based normativity must still be dealt with. And Chapter 3 forced the issue. It forged an internal link between Aboutness and evidential norms. Full-dress naturalism must speak to it.

Chapter 4 showed such normativity poses no principled difficulty. Its argument unearthed this version of Reliabilism:

(R) (a) If B is norm-based on perceptual evidence E such that **prob**(B/E) is Φ, and the fully norm-pruned evidence E* is such that **prob**(B/E*) remains Φ, then B is warranted;

(b) If B is norm-based on doxastic evidence E such that **prob**(B/E) is Φ, that evidence is warranted, and the fully norm-pruned evidence E* is such that **prob**(B/E*) remains Φ, then B is warranted;

(c) No other belief is warranted.

This view captures much in our pre-theoretic take on good reckoning. It forges an internal link between reason and content. It forges such a link between norms and the dynamics of thought. (R) is consistent with the view that warrant springs from content-based norm-guided reckoning.

Having said that, (R) does *not* say how norms must hook-up with truth to confer warrant. (R) is a schema. Φ is its placeholder for the chance-theoretic ground of evidential force. It's an open question if there is such a ground. We don't yet know if there's tight-enough fit between evidential force and chance to see the former as the latter. ([4.2] took up the question but left it open.) At this stage in our intellectual development, the reasonable position to adopt is Wait-and-See. Perhaps there is tight fit between evidential force and chance. Perhaps there is not. We don't yet know. Wait-and-See.

But even if we found perfect fit between Aboutness and nature, and even if we saw consciousness posed no principle difficulty for physicalism, and even if we found perfect fit between evidential force and nature, that would not secure physicalism. Zombies and Ghosts must be dealt with as well. They're perfectly conceivable. That looks to show they're genuinely possible. Many feel this refutes physicalism.

Chapter 5 shows that's too quick. There are two ways a claim can be conceivable. One is when full grasp of its content yields coherence. Another is when its content can be grounded in experiential imagination. Since it's coherent to mix Body and no Mind, Zombies are conceivable in the first sense. Since it's coherent to mix Mind and no Body, Ghosts are too. But only Ghosts can be grounded in experiential imagination. Zombies cannot. Their defining nature prevents such a cognitive grip on them.

Chapter 5 shows neither conceptual nor experiential conceivability is sufficient for genuine possibility. Rather, they are both defeasible evidence for it. We face three conceivability-based arguments for dualism. One springs from the conceptual conceivability of Zombies. One springs from the conceptual conceivability of Ghosts. And one springs from the experiential conceivability of Ghosts. As §5.5 made clear, though, the first two arguments traffic in defeated evidence.

While the conceptual possibility of Zombies is reason to think them genuinely possible, that reason is defeated by the conceptual possibility of their genuine *im*possibility. And while the conceptual possibility of Ghosts is reason to think them genuinely possible, that reason is defeated by the conceptual possibility of their genuine *im*possibility. The claims succumb to symmetric defeat. So we're left with one argument:

$$\mathcal{R}[G_{EI}]$$

(1g)*	$\oplus_{EI}G$	{Ghosts are experientially imaginable.}
(2g)*$^{\mathcal{R}}$	$\oplus_{EI}G \ni \blacklozenge G$	{Defeasibly: if ghosts are experientially imaginable, they're genuinely possible.}
(3g)	$\blacklozenge G \Rightarrow D$	{Ghosts are genuinely possible only if dualism is true.}
∴ (4g)	$\blacklozenge G$	{Ghosts are genuinely possible, from (1g)*&(2g)*$^{\mathcal{R}}$.}
∴ (5)	D	{Dualism is true, from (3g)&(4g).}

This argument fares better. Ghosts are experientially imaginable. That's reason to think them genuinely possible. The reason is not, however, defeated by conceptual possibility. Both (1g)* and (2g)*$^{\mathcal{R}}$ stand. Since (3g) also looks true – and especially so when it's re-emphasized that Ghosts are *unrealized* beings – $\mathcal{R}[G_{EI}]$ appears solid. It builds a case for dualism which physicalists have two ways to meet. They can find reason to defeat the evidential force of Ghosts' experiential imaginability. They can deny their genuine possibility entails dualism.

Current-day physicalists ground their view in a causal-based argument. It's statement varies from philosopher to philosopher. But the basic idea is simple:

[*]   The Overdetermination Argument

(1)   Mental events have macro spatial effects (e.g. arm movements).

(2)   Such effects are constituted by quantum spatial events (e.g. quantum tunnelling).

(3)   Every quantum spatial effect has a fully disclosive, purely quantum history.

(4)   For spatial events C, E and E*: if C causes E and E constitutes E*, then C causes E*.

(5)   The spatial effects of mental events are not generally overdetermined.

∴   (6)   Mental events are quantum events.

If [*] is sound, $\mathfrak{R}[G_{EI}]$ goes wrong. Either $(2g)^{\mathfrak{R}}$ deals in defeated evidence or (3g) is false.

As Chapter 6 made clear, though, [*] is far from sound. Only when large and small are conceptually homogeneous is it *obvious* causation rides atop spatial composition. Otherwise it's not obvious at all. In effect (4) assumes

(i)	large and small spatial properties are conceptually homogeneous,
(ii)	large spatial properties are bottom-up reductive, and
(iii)	large spatial change is bottom-up change.

But there's a Conceptual Gap between quantum and quotidian spatial fact. (i) is simply false. Further, (ii) and (iii) are exactly the kind of thing [*] sets out to prove, to wit, that micro-monism is true of reality. They beg the question. And to make matters worse, they're undermined by (i)'s falsity. The truth value of [*]'s false presupposition undercuts the viability of its question-begging presuppositions.

Similarly, [*] is meant to be causally univocal throughout. As I put it in §6.10: (5) aims to preclude effects standing on the catching end of a single relation twice over. This is meant to combine with (1)–(4) to entail (6). But the entailment requires quotidian and quantum causation are one. It requires they're the same relation writ to different levels of scale. In effect [*] assumes

(iv)	large and small causal relations are conceptually homogeneous,
(v)	large causal relations are bottom-up reductive, and
(vi)	large causal change is bottom-up change.

But here too we find a false assumption. Causal notions make no explicit appearance in quantum theory; and when they do show their face – say in orthodox discussion of measurement – the notions at work are probabilistic. Quotidian causation is conceptually deterministic. Quotidian and quantum causation are conceptually heterogeneous. (iv) is simply false. Further, (v) and (vi) are more of what [*] sets out to prove. They also beg the question. And they're undermined by (iv)'s falsity. Here too the truth value of a false presupposition undercuts the viability of question-begging ones.

Despite grounding the zeitgeist of our day, [*] does not withstand scrutiny. Its adherents outrun their headlights. Extant causal knowledge does not secure physicalism. Philosophers say it does time and again. But they shouldn't. The doctrine is nothing but dogma.

This doesn't mean our causal knowledge makes a case for dualism. It just leaves things open. The workings of the world as we know them are

consistent with physicalism and dualism. The reasonable position to adopt –
on their basis anyway – is Wait-and-See. Perhaps physics will regain conceptual homogeneity. Perhaps that will yield a sound overdetermination
argument. Then again, perhaps not. We don't yet know. Wait-and-See.

This leaves $\mathcal{R}[G_{EI}]$. Ghosts are experientially imaginable. That indicates
they're genuinely possible. (3g) says this entails dualism. We have a *prima
facie* case for that view.

But it too does not withstand scrutiny. As §6.11 made clear, the best
version of physicalism is modally modest. It does not assume property realization is modally invariant. It says nothing but this:

> (MP)   Mental properties are realized by physical properties. But
> that's contingently so. They might have been realized by
> non-mental properties. They might have been basic. In the
> latter case, mental properties would have genuinely con-
> tributed to the world. They would have belonged to the
> minimally complete description of things. They don't in
> fact do that; but they might have.

(MP) says our world is purely physical. It also says Mind could have been
basic. It's a modally modest view. It permits the genuine possibility of Ghosts.
But it denies that possibility entails dualism. (3g) is false. $\mathcal{R}[G_{EI}]$ is unsound.
The *prima facie* case is kaput.

What it means

The last lecture of *Naming and Necessity* stops with a footnote. Kripke ends
it by saying: 'I regard the Mind–Body Problem as wide open and extremely
confusing.' Chapters 1 to 6 speak to both halves of Kripke's remark. They
show he's exactly half right. The Mind–Body Problem is wide open. But it's
not so confusing after all.

What we must do is Wait-and-See. We must learn how the world works
out. We must discern whether it yields tight fit between Aboutness and
Nature. We must discern whether it yields such fit between evidential force
and Nature. If the answer is *yes* twiceover, Occam will side with the
physicalist. And nothing now known will override the support. Neither phenomenal consciousness nor the conceptual independence of Mind will trump
ontic savings. The reasonable position will be physicalism.

At present we're not in that position. We've no real grip on the fit between Aboutness and Nature; and we've no such grip on that between
evidential force and Nature. Perhaps they both align nicely. Perhaps they
don't. No one knows. At this stage in our intellectual development, the
reasonable position to adopt – on the Mind–Body Problem anyway – is
Wait-and-See.

'What's the take-home message of your book?', asked a good friend and colleague. 'The Wait-and-See view', I replied. 'Oh,' he said helpfully, 'you'll never get famous pushing *that* view.' Fair enough. But there's nothing to be done for it. The facts support the view. When it comes to the Mind–Body Problem, the reasonable position is Wait-and-See.

The road ahead

Chapters 1 to 6 contain two main hostages to fortune. I think they're secure as they stand. Otherwise I wouldn't have used them. But still: they *are* hostages to fortune. They should be tagged as such. They merit further scrutiny. They point the way to future work. Who knows? It might tip the balance. It might resolve the Mind–Body Problem.

The issues are simple to state. What's gone before assumes:

(I)   Concepts can have canonical links to evidence. When C is so linked to E, two things are true: application of C is *prima facie* warranted on the basis of E, and the E-to-C link is individuative of C. No concept could be C without being so warranted.

(II)   Genuine possibility is like genuine actuality. It's a realistic domain of fact. It does not spring from how we think. It does not spring from how we talk. We have no infallible guide to it from within. There can be slippage between conceptual and genuine possibility. The former does not entail the latter, not even in the ideal.

(I) played a key role in two spots. It helped diagnose the Explanatory Gap. It helped undermine the Overdetermination Argument. (II) helped dispel worries about Zombies and Ghosts. (I) and (II) are integral to what's gone before.

By my lights they are secure. Our concept of concept supports (I). Our concept of genuine possibility supports (II). But note well: the concepts here are *our* concepts. We've gleaned them from ordinary practice. And just as our daily concept of *what's* possible is blinkered – as §§6.8–9 made clear – so too our daily concept of possibility may be. Its realistic flavour may cut against a true link to be found between conceptual and genuine possibility. I do not believe that is so. But I'm by no means certain. After all, that belief is relatively pre-theoretical. It might turn out wrong on reflection. Similarly, our daily concept of concept may be blinkered as well. It's kinship with evidence may cut against a deep chasm to be found between them. I do not believe that is so. But again I am not certain.

Indeed: what's gone before suggests (I) and (II) should be prosecuted *alongside* the Mind–Body Problem. It suggests the topics are inexorably linked. We face three questions not one:

(A)   How do concepts and evidence relate?
(B)   How do conceptual and genuine possibility relate?
(C)   How do Mind and Body relate?

(A)–(C) should be prosecuted in tandem. That's one way to read this book. If (A) takes (I) and (B) takes (II) – as now seems likely – then (C) gets a deflationary answer: Wait-and-See. That's how I read it.

References

Albert, D. (1992) *Quantum Mechanics and Experience*. Harvard University Press.

Albert, D. and Loewer, B. (1988) 'Interpreting the Many Worlds Interpretation'. *Synthèse*.

Alston, W. (1999) 'Back to the Theory of Appearing'. *Philosophical Perspectives*.

Anderson, C. and Owens, J. (eds) (1990) *Propositional Attitudes*. Stanford University Press.

Aune, B. (1991) *Knowledge of the External World*. Routledge.

Austin, J. L. (1962) *Sense and Sensibilia*. Oxford University Press.

Ayer, A. J. (1936) *Language, Truth and Logic*. Victor Gollancz.

Ayer, A. J. (1973) *The Central Questions of Philosophy*. Weidenfeld and Nicolson.

Balog, K. (2000) 'New Conceivability Arguments or Revenge of the Zombies'. *The Philosophical Review*.

Bealer, G. (1982) *Quality and Concept*. Oxford University Press.

Bennett, J. (1988) *Events and Their Names*. Oxford University Press.

Block, N. (1990) 'Inverted Earth'. In Tomberlin (1990).

Block, N., Flanagan, O. and Guzeldere, S. (eds) (1996) *The Nature of Consciousness*. The MIT Press.

Block, N. and Stalnaker, R. (1999) 'Conceptual Analysis, Dualism, and the Explanatory Gap'. *The Philosophical Review*.

Brand, M. and Walton, D. (eds) (1976) *Action Theory*. Reidel.

Broad, C. D. (1925) *The Mind and Its Place in Nature*. London: Kegan Paul.

Burge, T. (1979) 'Individualism and the Mental'. In French, Ühling and Wettstein (1979).

Butchvarov, P. (1980) 'Adverbial Theories of Consciousness'. In French, Ühling and Wettstein (1980).

Cartwright, N. (1999) *The Dappled World*. Cambridge University Press.

Chalmers, D. (1996) *The Conscious Mind*. Oxford University Press.

Chalmers, D. (1998) 'Materialism and the Metaphysics of Modality'. *Philosophy and Phenomenological Research*.

Chisholm, R. (1957) *Perceiving*. Cornell University Press.

Chisholm, R. (1965) 'The Theory of Appearing'. In Swartz (1965).

Chisholm, R. (1970) 'Events and Propositions'. *Nous*.

Crane, T. (ed.) (1992) *The Contents of Experience*. Cambridge University Press.

Crane, T. (1995) 'The Mental Causation Debate'. *Proceedings of the Aristotelian Society*.

Cushing, J. (1998) *Philosophical Concepts in Physics*. Cambridge University Press.

Dancy, J. (ed.) (1988) *Perceptual Knowledge* (*Oxford Readings in Philosophy*). Oxford University Press.

David, M. (1994) *Correspondence and Disquotation*. Oxford University Press.

Davidson, D. (1970) 'Mental Events'. In Davidson (1980).

Davidson, D. (1980) *Essays on Actions and Events*. Oxford University Press.

Davidson, D. (1985) 'Reply to Quine on Events'. In LePore and Loewer (1985).

Davidson, D. (1993) 'Thinking Causes'. In Heil and Mele (1993).

Davidson, D. and Harman, G. (eds) (1970) *Semantics of Natural Language*. Reidel.

Davies, M. and Humberstone, L. (1980) 'Two Notions of Necessity'. *Philosophical Studies*.

Davies, M. and Humphreys, G. (eds) (1993) *Consciousness*. Basil Blackwell.

Descartes, R. (1911) *Meditations on First Philosophy or Principles of Philosophy*. In Haldane and Ross (1911).

Dretske, F. (1995) *Naturalising the Mind*. MIT Press.

Ducasse, C. J. (1942) 'Moore's Refutation of Idealism'. In Schilpp (1942).

Ehring, D. (1997) *Causation and Persistence*. Oxford University Press.

Evans, G. (1979) 'Reference and Contingency'. *The Monist*.

Evans, G. (1982) *The Varieties of Reference*. Oxford University Press.

Feldman, R. (1985) 'Reliability and Justification'. *The Monist*.

Field, H. (1977) 'Logic, Meaning and Conceptual Role'. *Journal of Philosophy*.

Field, H. (1996) 'The A Prioricity of Logic'. *Proceedings of the Aristotelian Society*.

Fodor, J. (1987) *Psychosemantics*. MIT Press.

Fodor, J. (1998) *Concepts*. Oxford University Press.

French, P., Ühling, T and Wettstein, H. (eds) (1979) *Midwest Studies in Philosophy IV: Studies in Epistemology*. University of Minnesota Press.

French, P., Ühling, T. and Wettstein, H. (eds) (1980) *Midwest Studies in Philosophy V: Studies in Epistemology*. University of Minnesota Press.

Gettier, E. (1963) 'Is Knowledge Justified Belief?' *Analysis*.

Goldman, A. (1967) 'A Causal Theory of Knowing'. *Journal of Philosophy*.

Goldman, A. (1979) 'What is Justified Belief?' In Pappas (1979).

Goldman, A. (1986) *Epistemology and Cognition*. Harvard University Press.

Goldman, A. (1988) 'Strong and Weak Justification'. *Philosophical Perspectives*.

Goldman, A. (1993) 'Epistemic Folkways and Scientific Epistemology'. *Philosophical Issues*.

Gunderson, K. (ed.) (1975) *Language, Mind and Knowledge: Minnesota Studies in the Philosophy of Science* VII. University of Minnesota Press.

Haldane, E. and Ross, G. (eds) (1911) *The Philosophical Works of Descartes*. Cambridge University Press.

Harman, G. (1990) 'The Intrinsic Quality of Experience'. In Tomberlin (1990).

Hart, B. (1988) *The Engines of the Soul*. Cambridge University Press.

Healy, R. (1989) *The Philosophy of Quantum Mechanics*. Cambridge University Press.

Heil, J. and Mele, A. (eds) (1993) *Mental Causation*. Oxford University Press.

Hill, C. (1981) 'Why Cartesian Intuitions Are Compatible with the Identity Thesis'. *Philosophy and Phenomenological Research*.

Hill, C. (1997) 'Imaginability, Conceivability, Possibility and the Mind–Body Problem'. *Philosophical Studies*.

Hill, C. (1998) 'Chalmers on the Apriority of Modal Knowledge'. *Analysis*.

Hill, C. and McLaughlin, B. (1998) 'There Are Fewer Things in Reality than Are Dreamt of in Chalmer's Philosophy'. *Philosophy and Phenomenological Research.*

Hinton, J. M. (1973) *Appearances.* Oxford University Press.

Honderich, T. (1982) 'The Argument for Anomolous Monism'. *Analysis.*

Hopkins, J. (1978) 'Mental States, Natural Kinds and Psychophysical Laws'. *Proceedings of the Aristotelian Society.*

Horwich, P. (1990) *Truth.* Basil Blackwell.

Horwich, P. (1998) *Meaning.* Oxford University Press.

Howard-Snyder, D. and F. (2000) 'Three Ecumenical Arguments for Infallibilism'. *Philosophy and Phenomenological Research.*

Hughes, R. I. G. (1989) *The Structure and Interpretation of Quantum Mechanics.* Harvard University Press.

Jackson, F. (1977) *Perception: A Representative Theory.* Cambridge University Press.

Jackson, F. (1982) 'Epiphenomenal Qualia'. *Philosophical Quarterly.*

Jackson, F. (1996) 'Mental Causation'. *Mind.*

Kaplan, D. (1978) 'On the Logic of Demonstratives'. *Journal of Philosophical Logic.*

Kaplan, D. (1979) 'Dthat'. *Syntax and Semantics.*

Kim, J. (1969) 'Events and Their Descriptions'. Reprinted in Kim (1993a).

Kim, J. (1973) 'Causation, Nomic Subsumption, and the Concept of an Event'. *Journal of Philosophy.* Reprinted in Kim (1993a).

Kim, J. (1976) 'Events as Property Exemplifications'. In Brand and Walton (1976). Reprinted in Kim (1993a).

Kim, J. (1993a) *Supervenience and Mind.* Cambridge University Press.

Kim, J. (1993b) 'Can Supervenience and "Non-Strict Laws" Save Anomalous Monism?' In Heil and Mele (1993).

Kim, J. (1996) *The Philosophy of Mind.* Westview Press.

Kim, J. (1997) 'The Mind–Body Problem: Taking Stock after Forty Years'. *Philosophical Perspectives.*

Kripke, S. (1980) *Naming and Necessity.* Harvard University Press. Originally published in Davidson and Harman (1970).

Langsam, H. (1997) 'The Theory of Appearing Defended'. *Philosophical Studies.*

Laurence, S. and Margolis, E. (1999) *Concepts: Core Readings.* MIT Press.

Leeds, S. (1978) 'Theories of Reference and Truth'. *Erkenntnis.*

LePore, E. and Loewer, B. (eds) (1985) *Action and Events: Perspectives on the Philosophy of Donald Davidson.* Basil Blackwell.

Levine, J. (1983) 'Qualia and the Explanatory Gap'. *Pacific Philosophical Quarterly.*

Levine, J. (1993) 'On Leaving Out What It's Like'. In Davies and Humphreys (1993).

Levine, J. (1997) 'Are Qualia Just Representations?' *Mind & Language.*

Levine, J. (1998) 'Conceivability and the Metaphysics of Mind'. *Nous.*

Lewis, D. (1966) 'An Argument for the Identity Theory'. *Journal of Philosophy.* Reprinted in Lewis (1983).

Lewis, D. (1973) 'Causation'. *Journal of Philosophy.* Reprinted with postscript in Lewis (1986a).

Lewis, D. (1979) 'Attitudes *de dicto* and *de se*'. *The Philosophical Review.*

Lewis, D. (1983) *Philosophical Papers*, Volume I. Oxford University Press.

Lewis, D. (1986a) *Philosophical Papers*, Volume II. Oxford University Press.

Lewis, D. (1986b) 'Events'. In Lewis (1986a).

Loar, B. (1990) 'Phenomenal States'. In Tomberlin (1990).

Loar, B. (1996) 'Phenomenal States (Second Version)'. In Block *et al.* (1996).

Loar, B. (1998) 'David Chalmers' *The Conscious Mind'*. *Philosophy and Phenomenological Research.*

Loewer, B. (1995) 'An Argument for Strong Supervenience'. In Savellos and Yalçin (1995).

Lombard, L. (1986) *Events.* Routledge.

MacDonald, G. (ed.) (1979) *Perception and Identity.* Macmillan.

Martin, M. G. F. (1998) 'Setting Things Before The Mind'. In O'Hear (1998).

McDowell, J. (1982) 'Criteria, Defeasibility and Knowledge'. *Proceedings of the British Academy.* Reprinted with revisions and additions in Dancy (1988).

McDowell, J. (1986) 'Singular Thought and the Extent of Inner Space'. In McDowell and Pettit (1986).

McDowell, J. (1994) *Mind and World.* Harvard University Press.

McDowell, J. (1995) 'Knowledge and the Internal'. *Philosophy and Phenomenological Research.*

McDowell, J. (1997) 'The 1997 Woodbridge Lectures'. *Journal of Philosophy.*

McDowell, J. and Pettit, P. (eds) (1986) *Subject, Thought and Context.* Oxford University Press.

McGinn, C. (1989) 'Can We Solve the Mind–Body Problem?' *Mind.*

McGinn, C. (1991) *The Problem of Consciousness.* Basil Blackwell.

McLaughlin, B. (1993) 'On Davidson's Response to the Charge of Epiphenomenalism'. In Heil and Mele (1993).

Mellor, H. (1995) *The Facts of Causation.* Routledge.

Merricks, T. (1995) 'Warrant Entails Truth'. *Philosophical and Phenomenological Research.*

Metzinger, T. (ed.) (1995) *Conscious Experience.* Ferdinand Schoningh.

Millikan, R. (1993) *White Queen Psychology.* MIT Press.

Millikan, R. (1997) 'Images of Identity: In Search of Modes of Presentation'. *Mind.*

Nagel, T. (1998) 'Conceiving the Impossible and the Mind–Body Problem'. *Philosophy.*

Noordhof, P. (1999) 'The Overdetermination Argument versus the Cause-and-Essence Principle: No Contest'. *Mind.*

O'Hear, A. (ed.) (1998) *Contemporary Issues in the Philosophy of Mind.* Cambridge University Press.

Papineau, D. (1993a) *Philosophical Naturalism.* Basil Blackwell.

Papineau, D. (1993b) 'Physicalism, Consciousness and the Antipathetic Fallacy'. *Australian Journal of Philosophy.*

Pappas, G. (ed.) (1979) *Justification and Knowledge.* Reidel.

Parret, H. and Bouveresse, J. (eds) (1981) *Meaning and Understanding.* De Gruyter.

Peacocke, C. (1979) *Holistic Explanation.* Oxford University Press.

Peacocke, C. (1983) *Sense and Content.* Oxford University Press.

Peacocke, C. (1995) *A Study of Concepts.* MIT Press.

Perkins, M. (1983) *Sensing the World.* Hackett Publishing Company.

Pessin, A. and Goldberg, S. (1996) *The Twin-Earth Chronicles.* M. E. Sharp.

Pollock, J. (1984) 'Justification and Reliability'. *Canadian Journal of Philosophy.*

Pollock, J. and Cruz, J. (1999) *Contemporary Theories of Knowledge* (2nd edition). Rowman & Littlefield.

Price, H. H. (1950) *Perception* (2nd edition). Methuen.

Putnam, H. (1975a) 'The Meaning of "Meaning"' in Gunderson (1975). Reprinted in Putnam (1975b).

Putnam, H. (1975b) *Mind, Language and Reality: Philosophical Papers* Vol. II. Cambridge University Press.

Putnam, H. (1994) 'The Dewey Lectures 1994: Sense, Nonsense, and the Senses – an Inquiry into the Powers of the Human Mind'. *Journal of Philosophy.*

Quine, W. v. O. (1969a) 'Epistemology Naturalized'. In Quine (1969b).

Quine, W. v. O. (1969b) *Ontological Relativity and Other Essays.* Columbia University Press.

Quine, W. v. O. (1970) *Philosophy of Logic.* Prentice Hall.

Quine, W. v. O. (1981) 'Things and Their Place in Theories'. In Quine (1985).

Quine, W. v. O. (1985) *Theories and Things.* Harvard University Press.

Rae, A. (1996) *Quantum Mechanics* (4th edition). Institute of Physics Publishing.

Robinson, H. (1994) *Perception.* Routledge.

Russell, B. (1912) *The Problems of Philosophy.* Oxford University Press.

Russell, B. (1914) 'The Relation of Sense-Data to Physics'. In Russell (1917).

Russell, B. (1917) *Mysticism and Logic.* Longmans & Co.

Russell, B. (1918) 'The Philosophy of Logical Atomism'. In Russell (1956).

Russell, B. (1927) *The Analysis of Matter.* Kegan Paul & Co.

Russell, B. (1948) *Human Knowledge: Its Scope and Limits.* George Allen & Unwin.

Russell, B. (1956) *Logic and Knowledge.* (Edited by Robert Marsh). George Allen & Unwin.

Ryle, G. (1949) *The Concept of Mind.* Hutchinson.

Salmon, N. (1986) *Frege's Puzzle.* MIT Press.

Salmon, N. (1989) 'Illogical Beliefs'. *Philosophical Perspectives.*

Savellos, E. and Yalçin, Ü. (eds) (1995) *Supervenience: New Essays.* Cambridge University Press.

Schiffer, S. (1981) 'Truth and the Theory of Content'. In Parret and Bouveresse (1981).

Schiffer, S. (1987a) 'The "'Fido'–Fido" Theory of Belief'. In *Philosophical Perspectives.*

Schiffer, S. (1987b) *Remnants of Meaning.* MIT Press.

Schiffer, S. (1990) 'The Mode-of-Presentation Problem'. In Anderson and Owens (1990).

Schilpp, P. A. (ed.) (1942) *The Philosophy of G. E. Moore.* Open Court Publishing.

Searle, J. (1983) *Intentionality.* Cambridge University Press.

Segal, G. (2000) *A Slim Book About Narrow Content.* MIT Press.

Sellars, W. (1975) 'The Adverbial Theory Of the Objects of Sensation'. *Metaphilosophy.*

Snowdon, P. (1981) 'Perception, Vision and Causation'. *Proceedings of the Aristotelian Society.* Reprinted in Dancy (1988).

Snowdon, P. (1992) 'How To Interpret "Direct Perception"'. In Crane (1992).

Sosa, E. (1964) 'The Analysis of "Knowledge that P"'. *Analysis.*

Sosa, E. (1993) 'Davidson's Thinking Causes'. In Heil and Mele (1993).

Stalnaker, R. (1978) 'Assertion'. *Syntax and Semantics.*

Strawson, P. F. (1979) 'Perception and Its Objects'. In MacDonald (1979).

Stubenberg, L. (1998) *Consciousness and Qualia.* John Benjamins.

Sturgeon, S. (1993) 'The Gettier Problem'. *Analysis.*

Sturgeon, S. (1999) 'Conceptual Gaps and Odd Possibilities'. *Mind.*

Swain, M. (1981) *Reasons and Knowledge.* Cornell University Press.

Swartz, R. (ed.) (1965) *Perceiving, Sensing and Knowing.* University of California Press.

Tomberlin, J. (ed.) (1990) *Philosophical Perspectives.* Ridgeview Publishing Company.

Tye, M. (1984) 'The Adverbial Approach to Visual Experience'. *Philosophical Review.*

Tye, M. (1992) 'Visual Qualia and Visual Content'. In Crane (1992).

Tye, M. (1995) *Ten Problems of Consciousness.* MIT Press.

Tye, M. (1999) 'Phenomenal Consciousness'. *Mind.*

Valberg, J. (1992) 'The Puzzle of Experience'. In Crane (1992).

Van Cleve, J. (1983) 'Conceivability and the Cartesian Argument for Dualism'. *Pacific Philosophical Quarterly.*

Van Gulick, R. (1993) 'Understanding the Phenomenal Mind: Are We All Just Armadillos?' In Davies and Humphreys (1993).

Van Gulick, R. (1995) 'What Would Count as Explaining Consciousness?' In Metzinger 1995.

Van Inwagen, P. (1978) 'Ability and Responsibility'. *Philosophical Review.*

Vendler, Z. (1967) *Linguistics and Philosophy.* Cornell University Press.

Wigner, E. (1967) *Symmetries and Reflections. Scientific Essays of Eugene P. Wigner.* Indiana University Press.

Witmer, G. (2000) 'Locating the Overdetermination Problem'. *British Journal for the Philosophy of Science.*

Yablo, S. (1993) 'Is Conceivability a Guide to Possibility?' *Philosophy and Phenomenological Research.*

Yablo, S. (1998) 'Concepts and Consciousness'. *Philosophy and Phenomenological Research.*

Zagzebski, L. (1996) *Virtues of the Mind.* Cambridge University Press.

Index